**To Renew Books
Phone (925) 969-3100**

your EIGHT-YEAR-OLD
Lively and Outgoing

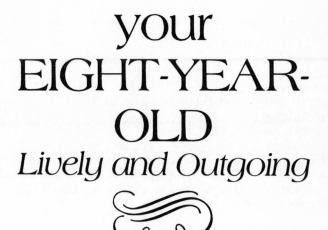

by Louise Bates Ames, Ph.D.
and Carol Chase Haber, M.D.
Gesell Institute of Human Development

Illustrated with photographs by Betty David

A Dell Trade Paperback

To Dr. Frances L. Ilg
Herself expansive and exuberant, lively and
outgoing, she provided many of our best
insights into the behavior of the child of eight.

CONTENTS

CONTENTS

your
EIGHT-YEAR-
OLD

chapter one
CHARACTERISTICS
OF THE AGE

The typical Eight-year-old can be described as outgoing, lively, and evaluative. Unlike the child at Seven, he does not withdraw when the going gets tough. On the contrary, he remains right out in front, meeting every challenge that life throws his way.

With his typically outgoing, *expansive* nature, an Eight-year-old is much more responsive to his environment than at Seven. With his high energy level, he seems willing to tackle almost anything, even the new and difficult. He is expanding emotionally, growing out of his earlier shyness, and relating to other people more easily than he used to. He even approaches strangers with some confidence.

Eight's liveliness, or *speed,* is obvious to almost any adult. He darts around the house or yard, seemingly unaware of physical obstacles in his path. His entire body seems ready for action. He works fast, plays fast (loves running games), talks fast, even eats fast. When necessary he can shift very rapidly from one activity to the next, and wastes little time in looking back.

Though at times his expansiveness and speed lead to carelessness, these usually don't cause the Eight-year-old too much difficulty. However, his *evaluativeness* certainly does. It makes him all too aware of his own failures. Eight tends to be hard on himself for his mistakes. His evaluativeness also makes him all too aware when other people do not respond as he would like them to. Eight is extremely sensitive to perceived criticism of others. On the other hand, this evaluativeness sometimes helps him make sound judgments as to what he can or cannot accomplish, when he is or isn't going to be successful. This helps to curb his headlong rush into things and can sometimes prevent him from undertaking the totally impossible.

Intellectually, as in other ways, Eight is becoming more expansive. He can express amazement and curiosity. He is growing aware of the impersonal forces of nature. He can distinguish fundamental similarities and differences when comparing a baseball and an orange, an airplane and a kite, wood and glass. The origin and growth of plants from seeds begins to intrigue him. He takes a deepening interest in the life processes of animals. He is even beginning to believe that all men are mortal and that even *he* will one day die. But at this relatively positive age, this knowledge does not depress him as it might have done earlier.

How Eight loves to talk! He comes home from school just "bursting" with news: "You never saw *anything* like it!" "Oh, it was *awful!*" In fact, everything tends to be dramatized: "Hey, what's the matter with me!" "This has got me crazy!" "I always get the easy ones wrong."

Personal space is expanding for the Eight-year-old. He can now return home alone by bus from a somewhat distant point. His walking area within his own neighborhood is so wide that it is sometimes hard to locate him. He loves to take trips to new cities, visit museums, zoos, and other places of interest. Eight's spatial world is expanding even further through an interest in geography. He has a fairly clear notion of points of the compass and different parts of his community in relation to each other.

The child at Seven tended to stick close to home. Eight explores new territory. He sees beyond the boundaries of his neighborhood. He likes to order from a mail-order catalog, loves to look things up in the encyclopedia.

Eight is in general healthier and less fatiguable than he was at Seven, more fond of rough-and-tumble play and boisterous games. His tempo is rapid when he talks, reads, writes, or practices the piano. He wolfs down food, sitting on the edge of his chair, ready to bolt outdoors without pulling up his socks or tucking in his shirt. Eight-year-old boys may add a little bravado to their slap-dash demeanor to emphasize their masculine toughness.

The Seven-year-old was in many ways, with his anxieties and dark suspicions, still very much a child. Eight seems to be moving toward adulthood. He is definitely growing up; he even looks more mature than he did at Seven. Subtle changes in Eight's body now hint at the body he is going to have when he gets older. He is much better coordinated when it comes to sports.

Relationships are extremely important at this age—the child's relationships with Mother and Father, with friends. At Six the child was busy building up practical working relationships with others. Now the girl or boy is building up emotional and attitudinal relationships. How he feels about others and how they feel about him is important.

The typical Eight-year-old tends to listen closely when adults talk among themselves. He watches their facial expressions; he hopes they may say something favorable about him, but he recognizes the gap between the world of the adult and his own world, and adjusts accordingly.

Eight is curious about and interested in human relationships, particularly those of the adults close to him. In fact, he can be described as downright nosy. Girls explore family problems and relationships through the medium of paper dolls. Like chessmen on a chessboard, the paper dolls symbolize agents and situations. Father, mother, bride, bridegroom, daughter, son, baby, visitor—all are represented by these dolls, which can be so freely manipulated with dramatic commentary. Sometimes the dialogue suggests more insight than the Eight-year-old can actually claim: "My husband would not be unfaithful to me!" said one dramatic Eight to her friend. "He has been already," the friend replied smugly.

Eight is increasingly aware of himself as a person, is interested in what makes him tick. As one mother of an

Eight-year-old remarked, "Even his gestures are like him." Now the child is conscious of his own appearance, his own personal qualities. He may be torn between the desire to grow up and the wish to remain as he is. And in his dramatic way he exaggerates his problems and dilemmas.

Eight's performance is often only mediocre, and his notion of other people's standards is extremely high. This discrepancy leads to tears and temporary unhappiness, at times; or Eight may boast and alibi to make up for what he can do and what he would like to do. His feelings are easily hurt, and the child of this age tends to be extremely sensitive to criticism. He is quick to recognize his all-too-frequent failures and will groan: "I never get anything right!" "I always do things wrong!"

While Eight is hard on himself, he is also hard on others. He can be quarrelsome and aggressive toward people, particularly Mother. To excuse his attacks on others, he often convinces himself that he himself is being attacked.

Eight's sensitivity is also revealed in his need for praise for what he's done. "This is crummy, isn't it?" he may ask, hoping to be assured that it's great. He is, however, rather discriminating, so that the praise he seeks must be at least partially plausible.

When things go very wrong for Eights, they do get truly angry. Some show their anger at least partly in jest. Thus they may tense up their faces in exasperation, project their lower jaws, and draw back and flex their arms at the elbow as they clench their fists. This dramatic pose is sure to produce laughter from other children at school.

Eight is becoming more responsible in regard to time. His increased speed in action makes him less vulnerable to the demands of time. He can now be expected to arrive at school at the proper hour. However, some Eights do not tell time as well as they did earlier; Eights are often careless with their watches and may lose, break, or misplace them. Though he may tell time less well, Eight is aware of punc-

tuality. He keeps himself posted by asking others what time it is. If he knows he is going to arrive home late, he may even be responsible enough to telephone.

As at other ages, parents may find it useful to locate their Eight-year-old in relation to the ever-alternating stages of equilibrium and disequilibrium, of inwardized and out wardized behavior. As Figure 1 suggests, we place Eight on the equilibrium side of the spiral. This may seem strange in view of the fact that we have described the child of this age as an often difficult little person. True, Eights can be extremely troublesome at times, especially in relation to Mother. Along with his expansive exuberance, his love of the dramatic, the Eight-year-old often seems to be enjoying himself even as he suffers; though he may criticize himself, basically he feels pretty good about himself.

There is no question as to where the Eight-year-old belongs on the spiral of alternating periods of inwardized and outwardized behavior. As Figure 2 illustrates, it is squarely on the side of expansiveness.

DISEQUILIBRIUM   **EQUILIBRIUM**

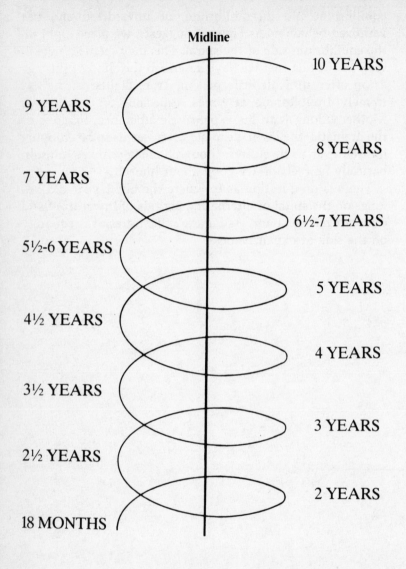

Figure 1
Alternation of Ages of Equilibrium and Disequilibrium

INWARDIZED BEHAVIOR

OUTWARDIZED BEHAVIOR

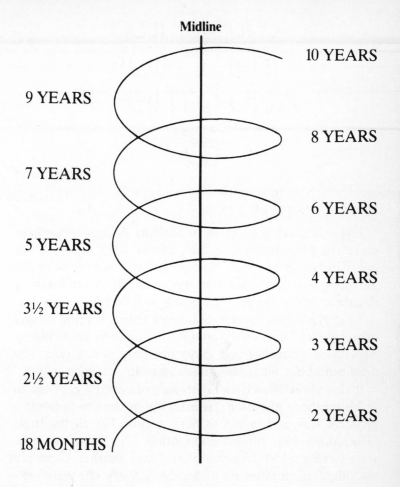

Midline

10 YEARS

9 YEARS

8 YEARS

7 YEARS

6 YEARS

5 YEARS

4 YEARS

3½ YEARS

3 YEARS

2½ YEARS

2 YEARS

18 MONTHS

Figure 2
Alternation of Ages of Inwardized and Outwardized Behavior

chapter two
THE CHILD
AND OTHERS

MOTHER—CHILD RELATIONS

The relationship of child to Mother at Eight is perhaps more complex, intriguing, and intense than at any other age. This must be clearly understood if a mother hopes to get along with her child in everyday life or in any teaching situation where she may be trying to help him.

Your typical Eight-year-old, more than the child of any other age, is "all mixed up with" his mother. He is highly dependent upon her and cares not only about what she does but about what she thinks as well.

It almost seems as if an Eight-year-old cannot get enough of his mother's attention. He is highly possessive of her in a physical way and wants to hang around her all the time. "He haunts me," reports one mother. "It's almost as if he were having a love affair with me," says another. Certainly any Eight is quite aware of Mother's every change of expression, her every mood. Some express real jealousy of their mother—of any time or attention she gives to anybody else.

The Six-year-old wants his mother to do what *he* wants her to. The Eight-year-old wants her to *want* to do what he wants her to.

At Six, it is enough if Mother simply goes through the

motions. Thus Mother can pretend she and her daughter are ladies writing letters, and can actually write "real" letters of her own as they play. At Eight, such superficiality and pretense simply will not do.

Now there must be constant interaction, and Mother's full attention is demanded as they play. This interaction requires almost constant *conversation* as well as action.

If not occupied in imaginative play, Eight likes to engage in endless board and dice or card games, which so many at this age dearly love and of which many mothers so quickly tire.

The late Haim Ginott once replied to a mother who complained to him about this endless game playing: "Where is it written that a mother has to be an entertainment committee?" Unfortunately for the weary parent, it is written is in the laws of growth.

It is important to the growing child that his mother share

intimately in his thoughts, imaginings, conversations, and games. To make this strong interpersonal relationship a satisfactory one, it's important for Mother to sacrifice quite a lot of her time and energy.

If this relationship goes smoothly, most Eights will naturally, at Nine, move away from Mother to satisfactory relationships with others. If the relationship is not satisfactory, this major disappointment may lie at the root of later unfulfilling interpersonal relationships.

As the level of communication desired by the Eight-year-old child is *so* intense, it is our recommendation that Mother limit the amount of time she and her child will play together. During that time, it works best if she can devote her entire attention to the child. Mothers can talk things over with their Eight-year-old and explain that they wish they could spend more time playing or talking but that since they have many other commitments, this isn't possible. They can then tell the child that they are going to spend half an hour a day (or whatever amount of time can be spared) with just the two of them doing things together. This block of time should be set aside and Mothers should try to concentrate fully on their son or daughter.

A little boy who had raked up all the leaves on the front lawn was visibly disappointed when his busy mother, hurrying into the house with her groceries, did not notice or comment on his raking. Whenever possible, it is worth trying to satisfy Eight's demands for attention. This will help him during this needy age and make it easier for independence at Nine. And remember, there is a certain amount of reciprocity here. The child of this age wants his mother to live up to *his* demands, but he also wants to satisfy hers, to live up to her standards for him.

What complicates matters, however, is that while Eight demands a great deal from his mother, he is at the same time more resistant to her than he was earlier. He obeys best if she puts things just the "right" way. Thus he often prefers a gentle hint to a command. A wink or a nod sometimes does the trick. Or, for example, saying the word "hands" rather than asking Eight straight out to wash his hands may be effective. (This kind of communication seems to make the child feel that he has a special secret with his mother.)

All too often, when asked to do something, the child gives some excuse such as "I'm busy" or "Well, I'll do it later." At this age it may be better to give him his time, for he usually *does* obey requests if allowed to come to them on his own terms. Eight is less forgetful than just a year earlier.

There is considerable use of the question "What?" at Eight. A boy or a girl can look right at Mother as she gives a command, can seem to hear her, but then ask "What?" Attention shifts so quickly that the child forgets what you say almost as you say it.

Though Eight dearly loves his mother, and in fact is very free with physical expressions of affection, he may become so furious with her that he says with real venom, "You're a skunk." He is highly aware of the mistakes other people make, especially his mother, and will point them out to her. He's sensitive about his own shortcomings as well, and when things go wrong, or if Mother makes even a modest criticism, Eight may attack: "So you're against me too."

It's important to remember that the intensity of Eight's relationship with his mother has its good side as well as its bad. It is often possible to use Eight's almost insatiable demand for his mother's time and attention to initiate what the adult may consider useful or educational activities.

The wise mother will suggest that any reading-related or other school-related tasks are something fun and nice they are going to do together. Eight is not a good self-starter, but once started he will need a certain amount of freedom to do things his own way. (But freedom or not, he likes Mother to be right there in attendance.) Also, he tires of the activity fairly early on and may need Mother's help in holding up until work time is over.

If fatigue brings on an outburst of temper when mother and child are working together (as on homework), it is wise to terminate the situation or at least to give a little recess.

Mother should be lavish with her praise when child has even a small success, though as Eight can to some extent evaluate his own performance, praise needs to be both reasonable and realistic. As noted in Chapter 1, the child of this age often fishes for praise. While drawing, he may comment, "That's terrible, isn't it?" One hopes that Mother can find something about the drawing that she can truthfully praise.

FATHER—CHILD RELATIONS

Eight's relationship with Father tends to be less intense and therefore as a rule smoother than his relationship with Mother.* Eight enjoys Father's company but does not demand his undivided attention as he does with Mother. Nor is he as insistent that his father speak or think in a certain way, and will even allow him to make a mistake now and then. Eight gives less ardent expressions of affection to Father but also is easier on him and usually minds him better than Mother.

Certainly most Eights respect their father's authority and tend to obey his commands without argument, though they may mumble a bit when he is out of hearing. Eight's mother may be in the center of his universe, but he probably admires his father more.

As Eight is not as emotionally entangled with Father as with Mother, some of a child's most enjoyable times may

---

* This is true in a two-parent family. In a one-parent family where the mother is absent and the father is the caretaker, many of the intense responses that Eights normally have to their mothers may indeed be seen with the father.

come when the two of them are together. It is because things are usually less emotional between them that Father may be effective in stepping in and settling disputes when child and Mother are having a difficult time, as is so often the case.

However, things are not always smooth. Fathers more than mothers object to many of the child's ways of behaving—the noisy, rough, careless, sloppy behavior, the poor table manners, daydreaming, dramatics.

The Eight-year-old is highly aware of the relationship between his or her parents. Earlier he may seem to have assumed that all was well even in the face of considerable evidence to the contrary. Now Eights may worry about their parents' relationship if they do not seem to be getting on well. Conversely, if they are getting on well, an Eight may be jealous of their relationship. (It is often hard to satisfy the Eight-year-old!)

Family is very important to the child at this age, and Eights tend to be extremely curious about all that is going on—phone calls, correspondence, conversation. Eight seems to be trying to find his place in relation to the adult world in general and to his parents in particular. This is often hard for him to do. At Seven the child seemed to be building up his concept of family. Now he is trying to make it work, and this is not always easy for him.

Children at Eight are very quick to pick up on their parents' attitudes, not only toward them but toward things in general. They are especially aware of and influenced by their parents' attitudes toward such matters as race, religion, the opposite sex. They often observe more than we think they do.

RELATIONS WITH SIBLINGS

One thing that complicates Eight's relationship with siblings is the intensity of his relationship with his mother. He tends to be jealous of her, especially jealous of time and attention she may devote to other children in the family. Also, a girl or boy of this age tends to be overaware of slights or imagined insults.

Thus by his very nature Eight often has difficulty with siblings even when they themselves are peaceful in intent. Unfortunately, some Eights are reported to be consistently bad with siblings—teasing, being selfish, quarreling. Eight, with his basically outgoing nature, finds it hard not to get involved with anyone around him, including siblings. And as the behavior of other people seldom meets his expectations, much friction ensues.

Eight tends to dramatize. Thus squabbles with siblings,

as he reports them to his parents, tend to be vastly exaggerated.

An Eight loves to argue and picks up on other people's mistakes. This is tiresome to older siblings. Moreover, at Eight the child does not want younger siblings tagging along; and his or her company is not often welcomed by older siblings.

Some areas of behavior do show improvement. The child can now take part in competitive games and can often lose without going all to pieces. But with his antenna out to be sure that he gets his fair share, he often feels that siblings are getting more privileges than he. The typical Eight-year-old wants *all* the privileges that any other siblings have (even those considerably older) and fears that siblings may put something over on him.

As at other ages, the quality of the relationship does depend to a marked extent on the ages of the siblings. With those Five and under, Eight may be reasonably patient and tolerant. However, when responsible for the care of a younger sibling, he is likely to be too strict. He does best when he is told ahead of time exactly how to behave. Then he likes to hear later how well he has done.

Siblings between Six and Ten may be too close to his own age to permit harmony. Eight all too easily gets down to the level of those just younger. He has lost the "big brother" attitude that he practiced at Seven and may quickly get involved in teasing and fighting.

Eight-year-olds get on badly, as a rule, with Eleven-year-olds, who get on badly with almost everyone. They may even have difficulty with Twelves, who get on well with siblings of most other ages.

But they do tend to get on reasonably well with any brothers and sisters over Twelve, who tend either to be relatively patient with them or to ignore them.

One interesting, though by no means surprising, aspect of sibling relationships occurs when Eight takes out his

frustration at another person on a sibling. As one mother asked her Eight-year-old son, "Why do you hit your sister when it's me you're mad at?"

RELATIONS WITH GRANDPARENTS

Eight's relationship with grandparents depends to some extent on whether they live in the household, as often used to be the case, or, as is more likely nowadays, in their own house or apartment. If they are part of the household, Eight may at times be quite rude and aggressive, involving Grandma (less often Grandpa) in his tangles with the family.

The difference in Eight's reaction to the two of them may be due to the fact that grandfathers tend not to intrude themselves in family squabbles. Grandmothers often do. If Grandma is a part of the household, it may be wise for her to relate to the child only through some specific channel, such as playing games or reading. The worst time for her to intervene is when the child's father and mother are handling him. Then any interference from Grandmother is likely to bring forth some very uncomfortable and rude remarks from all concerned.

However, when grandparents are merely visiting, or when Eight is visiting them, the relationship is usually quite delightful. Eight's eyes may still shine as they did when he was younger at the very sight of beloved grandparents.

Time spent together can be altogether delightful, enjoyed fully by both generations. Many Eights, like children of other ages, feel that they can confide (even misdeeds or difficulties) to grandparents, who will understand, sympathize, and not punish. The relationship still takes on the aspect of a mutual admiration society. The child of this age seems to appreciate the more or less unconditional affection his grandparents feel for him.

Many grandparents, more than parents (at least on a short-term basis), are able to devote the long periods of play and close interaction that Eight so loves and needs. As one Eight-year-old explained it, "I love them because they give me things and play with me and take me places."

Girls at this age describe their grandmothers in terms of her hair, or say that she is "nice." They describe their grandfathers in terms of hair or lack of hair, or in terms of activities, such as "He reads the paper and watches TV." Boys describe their grandmothers in terms of hair, age, glasses; their grandfathers in terms of his age, hair, type of work, or say he is "nice" or "fun."

FAMILY RELATIONS

As each child's behavior is influenced by his basic individuality, stage of development, and environment, special mention should be made of the influence of the most important part of his environment—his family.

To begin with, the number of children in a family strongly influences the extent to which the family is influenced by and responsive to the child's succeeding stages of behavior. When there is only one child, each stage is apt to strike his or her parents with extremely forceful impact. When a first child creeps, says his first word, takes a first step, all of these activities are duly noted and admired. That second or third children will eventually creep and talk and walk is pretty much taken for granted.

The stages of behavior that occur at succeeding ages will similarly be met with wonder by parents of first children. A first child's negativism at Two and one-half, insecurity at Three and one-half, out-of-bounds behavior at Four, "Try and make me" or "I hate you" rebelling at Six, withdrawal at Seven, and speedy, expansive, and evaluative behaviors at Eight each may be given full sway. Such behavior may indeed dominate a household and often cause serious concern to parents, who wonder why their child is behaving as he does.

By the time a second, third, or fourth child expresses these same behaviors, parents have seen it all before. In addition, in a big family there is often not enough time, space, or emotional energy to allow anybody to pay too much attention to the changing stages of behavior unless they are very extreme. These stages still occur, but even a very demanding child will go only so far if his antics attract minimal attention.

Not only does the number of children vary from household to household, but nowadays even the basic family structure itself is not uniform. According to an article in the August 15, 1983, issue of *Behavior Today*, in 1970, 85 percent of children in this country lived in a two-parent family. In 1980, this number had dropped to 75 percent. These figures vary greatly according to race. According to *Behavior Today*'s 1980 figures, 80 percent of white children but only 47 percent of black lived with both parents. More recent figures are even more discouraging.[1]

Any child growing up in a single-parent family, or in a stepfamily, may do well to survive emotionally, let alone expect the luxury of having his stages of behavior recognized and respected. Thus an Eight-year-old being brought up by Mother alone may make even greater emotional demands of her than he would have were both parents present in the household.

How the mother responds to this often excessive demand may vary. If she is under incredible pressures to support her family, she may very well be even less able to meet Eight's emotional demands than if the child's father were present. On the other hand, if financial pressures are not excessive and if the mother has time, she may be able to satisfy the child's demands more fully than she might have in a two-parent family.

Or perhaps Father is the single parent. Then some of the emotional demands customarily made of Mother may now be focused on him.

If the family is a stepfamily, a child's development may be treated in a similar fashion to the way it would be in a family with several children. It's one thing to overcome the hurdles of one's own child's behavioral development. It is almost sure to be harder with a stepchild. Thus in a large family, or in a stepfamily, some of the quite significant changes in behavior that come with age may go more or less unnoticed or ignored.

The special needs of the ever-demanding Eight-year-old will, in all likelihood, be met most fully in a not-too-large, moderately prosperous two-parent family in which both parents are the child's biological parents. This is the case whether the mother works outside the home or not. In contrast, when a family is struggling to get by from day to day, a child's emotional needs may of necessity be given a very low priority.

CHILDREN JUDGE US TOO

"Do you think grownups like children?" we asked an Eight-year-old of our acquaintance.

"No, I don't think so," he replied.

"Surely your Mom likes you," we insisted.

"Yes," he admitted, "Mom does. But I'm not too sure about Dad."

"I bet your Dad likes you too," we persisted.

"Well, yes, maybe. He *is* helpful. And of course he works and makes the money so we can live."

This line of inquiry seeming fruitful, we continued our questions. "How about Grandma and Granddad?"

"Oh, I know they like us because they always bring us presents."

One more question: "How about your great-grandma?"

"Oh, she hates kids" was his reply. "She says they are noisy and tiresome and they break things."

Most of us have our own ideas about how *we* feel about children—it's to be hoped that most of us like them. We found it interesting, and you might too, to find out what *your* children think about you and other grownups.

RELATIONS WITH FRIENDS

Outgoing Eight tends to have a goodly number of friends and considerable enthusiasm for friendship. The typical Seven-year-old was principally concerned with himself and how other people treated him. Eight has gone a step farther

in dealing with others. He is interested not just in how people treat him but in his *relationship* with others. He is ready for, and wants, a good two-way relationship. Furthermore, it is not just what people do that concerns him but also what they think. He has more to give to other people than he did earlier, but he also expects more of them in return. Eight is much less of a tattletale than earlier because he *wants* things to go well between himself and his friends.

This is an age at which, even if they have not done so earlier, many a girl or boy now has a "best" friend. The relationship between these friends may be very close and demanding; there tends to be much arguing, disputing, "getting mad." The quality of the relationship between two children, not simply what they do together, is becoming important in the eyes of the Eight-year-old. Much more social rapport may be shown now than earlier and more effort to cooperate with other children and to conform to the demands of others. At any rate, Eight wants to be happy and would like to have his friends happy too.

In spite of the complexity and intensity of these relationships, the trend is toward longer periods of relatively peaceful play with others, with only minor verbal disagreements. However, any unsupervised play session may end in disagreement or in the disgruntled departure of at least one participant.

Friendship is a strong concept now but the word "enemy" is often used, and this is an age when successful and popular children are all too likely to pick on any ugly duckling.

There is often much less playing with children of the opposite sex at Eight. Children may play best with others of their same sex and more or less their same age. Some Eights, however, play best with older children. Eight is apt to admire an older child of Twelve, and this older child will often in turn protect his admirer from being bullied or mistreated by others. A few Eights, who earlier had difficulty in approaching other children, may now make awkward attempts to interest another child.

Eight now figures strongly in neighborhood group play, especially in athletic activities, either organized or unorganized. Leaders are beginning to stand out. This may also be a time for the beginning of informal "secret" clubs, though with most children this does not go very far.

However, for all we may generalize, it is important to keep in mind that there are few areas in which individual differences show themselves more clearly than in the matter of friendships. Some Eight-year-olds seem always surrounded by friends; the phone always rings; the house seems always full of friends; or they are out visiting. Friendship comes easily, effortlessly. At the opposite extreme is the boy or girl who only with great effort makes a single friend. And if that friend moves away, it may be a long time before a replacement is found.

Unfortunately, finding a friend for your child is one thing that you as a parent cannot do too much about, and it is something that troubles many parents a great deal. In fact, parents often worry about a child's lack of friends more than the child himself does. It can help parents if they realize that not all children have an equal need of friends.

The quiet, diffident child whom we describe as an ectomorph often will not be the center of a large social group at any time in his life. Such a child may be quite comfortable with his own company—reading, watching television, studying, doing science experiments or working with a computer, playing with a pet. He does not go out of his way to seek out other people. One best friend may be all he wants or needs.

The more active, muscular mesomorph, with his outgoing, vigorous ways, tends to be popular—in fact, tends to be a leader. Other children flock to him and follow him. Such a boy or girl is likely to be a good athlete and thus much admired for athletic prowess. He or she seldom lacks for friends. These friendships may make up in number for what they lack in intensity of relationship.

Nor does the round, friendly endomorph lack for friendship. He sincerely likes people, likes having them around, enjoys their company, and they enjoy his. People are comfortable with this kind of child, who would rather be popular than to be a leader or to have his own way.

Parents *can* help a little, even with an Eight-year-old. They certainly can't make friends for their child, or force other children to play with him, but often they can invite some other child to accompany them on family outings, or can see that their boy or girl takes part in organized club activities such as Cub Scouts or Brownies or Indian Guides. Some children who are not entirely successful in unorganized play do best in a more structured situation with an adult in charge.

chapter three
ROUTINES, HEALTH, AND TENSIONAL OUTLETS

EATING

Parents who up till now have been discouraged because their boy or girl "never eats a thing" are now pleased at the child's typically increasing appetite. Most children at Eight have a very good appetite. Normally good eaters now often seem to be ravenously hungry. As one mother put it, "He eats like a hog, just shovels it in." And even the poorest and least enthusiastic eaters are now improving.

Most now not only eat large quantities, but eat very rapidly, so that some even get to third helpings before a meal is finished. Parents may actually need to restrict the amount eaten, as some Eights experience excessive weight gains.

Children of this age tend to increase the number of foods they will eat. We say of Six-year-olds that they want both chocolate and vanilla ice cream, being unable to choose either one and stick to their choice. Sevens always want whatever is their specially preferred flavor. But Eights will eat any kind, or perhaps several kinds mixed together.

Eight still has food dislikes. He cannot understand, for instance, why "they had to spoil that beautiful ham with that awful cream sauce." The child's appraisal of food may be influenced by his sense of smell. The smell of peanut butter may repel him, or it may produce a glow of pleasure. This use of smell to decide whether or not the child likes a certain kind of food can be extremely aggravating to parents. (One mother we know, as her son put his nose down to smell his food, obeyed her impulse and pushed his face right down onto his plate. We do not recommend this— although her impulse was understandable!)

Most Eights are adventurously ready to taste almost anything, though many do not like fat on meat. Parents should be very careful not to force foods on their child because he may actually be allergic to the refused food. (On the other hand, an allergic child may actually prefer the food that is so bad for him. Parents today are much more aware of the possibility that a child may be allergic to certain foods than they were in the past. They also know that offending foods may not only affect the child's physical health but also his behavior.)[1,2,3,4]

The child of Eight usually handles table implements fairly well, though some do hold fork and spoon pronately, which results in a pushing rather than a scooping manipulation. Fingers are used much less than formerly. Most Eights, though not all, can now cut their meat with a knife.

Table manners are improving, though there is a definite contrast between table manners at home and away. If a parent becomes too discouraged with the Eight-year-old at home, we suggest taking him to a restaurant, or inviting a friend over for a meal. Then things pick up.

At home, admittedly, all too many Eights bolt their food or gobble or shove it into their mouth, spill it, push it around on the plate, take too-big mouthfuls, talk with their mouth full. They are apt to play with their silverware and reach across the table for food. While at this age children are aware of good table manners (and may actually keep an eye on Father to see if he notices what they are doing), they find it hard to put good manners into practice. They talk and argue a lot and are likely to interrupt adults.

Their speedy eating adds a special complication to a sometimes already difficult situation: Many find themselves ready for dessert long before the rest of the family is ready. If dessert does not come soon enough, it may be wise to let them leave the table and come back when it is ready. Otherwise they are apt to get into trouble, especially with siblings.

Individual Differences: It is important for any parent, in adjusting his or her own expectations as to how much and how "well" a child should eat, to appreciate that there tend to be tremendous individual differences from one child to another in response to food. There are some—the round, plumpish endomorphs—who love food. They live for it, are always eating, never can seem to get enough. Even when not eating they like to be doing something with their mouths—chewing gum, sucking at a lollypop. Such children are never considered feeding problems. The difficulty is not to get them to eat but to get them to curb their eating. Such children often have serious weight problems, and thus their intake needs to be watched.

At the opposite extreme are the thin, angular ectomorphs. Such children, thin but not underweight, often seem almost entirely uninterested in food. Parents of these children worry a great deal, and often unnecessarily, that their children are not eating enough to keep them alive. The truth is that not only their feeding interest but actually their feeding needs are very modest. As long as they seem healthy and their pediatrician is not concerned about them, parents will do best not to nag at them about their eating.

Parents should try not to worry about quantity of food consumed. *Quality,* however, is something else again. Another tremendous individual difference with regard to food has to do with the foods a child can and cannot tolerate.

Most parents have always tried to feed their children properly, to see that they were well nourished. However, in years past, this usually did not go much beyond being sure that every child, every day, had at least something from each of the four basic food groups: fruit and vegetables, carbohydrates, protein, and dairy products.

Nowadays not only pediatricians but also many parents are much more sophisticated about the whole area of nourishment. We have become increasingly aware that many children are highly allergic to certain foods. Most everyone recognizes the fact that a food or drink or even medicine is bad for a child if it causes him to wheeze and sneeze, have difficulty breathing, or break out in spots. What has only recently been recognized (and this is still not accepted by everyone) is that *foods to which a child is allergic can also adversely influence behavior.*

All too many children cannot tolerate such quite ordinary foods as milk, citrus fruits, cheese, chocolate, wheat products, and, above all, sugar. Eating such foods may make them physically ill. Or, even more subtle and dangerous, it can adversely affect their behavior. Though not everyone as yet agrees, it is generally believed that foods the child cannot tolerate can cause hyperactivity, learning disabilities, and other undesirable behavior.

And not only are some foods not tolerated by some children, but many children need certain foods or food supplements (vitamins, minerals, other substances) that their bodies lack. Getting just the right balance—omitting harmful foods and furnishing any food supplements needed—is a tricky business. But those parents who have achieved a good balance, either with the help of their physician or by their own trial and error, have found it well worthwhile in terms of improved behavior and a healthier as well as a happier child.

See notes, page 143, for books by William Crook, Leo Galland, Lendon Smith, and Ray C. Wunderlich and Dwight K. Kalita for helpful suggestions about improving your child's diet.

SLEEPING

The bedtime hour is inevitably growing later. Most Eights now start for bed sometime between eight and nine P.M., though for most it takes at least half an hour or maybe even more before the child is finally settled down. Whatever the hour determined by the parent, most Eights are not quite ready for it when the time comes. Most want to finish whatever game they may be playing or read "just one more chapter."

Reasonable firmness on the part of the parent is important here. Some mothers permit the child to watch a favorite TV program if he gets ready for bed first.

Most can get ready for bed by themselves but still want to be tucked in. Some read for a while before saying their good nights, some need only a brief "good night," others still enjoy a chatting time. (A few extremely independent children can undress, take a bath, open their window, turn out the light, and go to bed entirely by themselves without the usual good night from Mother, but these are in the minority.)

Some go to sleep rather quickly after the light is out. Others lie awake for half an hour or so. Sleep is usually sound. Many Eights are "wonderful" sleepers just as they are said to be "wonderful" eaters. Most probably dream, but this is not a big age for nightmares. Few need to get up for toileting, but if they do, they can take care of this themselves.

Ten is an average number of hours for sleep, with most Eights waking between seven and seven-thirty in the morning.

Individual Differences: Though individual differences in sleep needs are probably much greater in adults than in children, when thinking about how much sleep children need it's important to keep in mind that not everybody is "average." In adults, sleep needs often vary from those people who can manage very nicely on five hours a night, to those who need eight and would enjoy nine. Parents probably suffer most from those preschoolers who need very little sleep, children who are out of bed at five or six in the morning, needing attention. By Eight years even the early risers can usually keep themselves busy without bothering their parents.

Other big differences occur in relation to the ease of getting to sleep. There are many children who go to sleep almost the minute they hit the pillow. These tend to be the strongly built muscular children whom we class as meso-morphs. Endomorphs, too, those plump, round children who love their beds, usually curl up and go to sleep without too much difficulty.

Ectomorphs (thin, angular children) have more difficulty. These are boys and girls who seem to resist change and transition, so that the transition from waking to sleep and, in the morning, from sleep to waking, is difficult. Such children often lie awake for an hour or more before they can manage to get to sleep. Often they worry about this wakefulness. Some solve the problem by reading to themselves (either with or without parental permission). Others find that a radio can help fill in this wakeful period pleasantly.

In the mornings, such children often need a little warning ahead of time before they are going to need to get out of bed. They cannot leap out of bed, fully awake, as do their more strongly built brothers and sisters.

BATHING AND DRESSING

Eights' bathing habits vary a great deal. Some are considerably more independent than they were a year earlier, but others, with their strong demand for Mother's constant presence, may like a little more help than they preferred at Seven.

Many initially resist their bath as they may other matters of domestic routine, but once in, most enjoy it. They like the feel of warm water on their skin. They enjoy sliding back and forth in the tub. A boy may pretend that he is a submarine. Most are not required to bathe daily—two or three times a week satisfies most parents.

Many Eights are not particularly fussy about their neck, ears, or back because they can't see them. Some can shampoo their own hair and can cut fingernails on their nondominant hand. Keeping fingernails cut very short is the best way to keep them clean.

A few Eight-year-olds, probably more girls than boys, spontaneously wash their hands before meals, but most need and accept reminding with only a trace of resistance. Many give hand washing only a lick and a promise, wiping most of the dirt off on the hand towel.

Eight-year-olds can, of course, dress themselves, and most do so with relative ease and speed. Most do not get sidetracked along the way as may have been the case at Seven. However, a certain amount of supervision may be needed as many Eights are remarkably messy. Shirts or blouses are not tucked in, buttons are left unbuttoned, even zippers may be left unzipped.

Most can now choose their own clothes each morning, more or less appropriate with regard to season, weather, occasion. A few if left entirely on their own may turn up without any underwear or with two different colored socks, but most do reasonably well. Eights prefer to make their own choices and not to have clothes laid out for them by their mother.

Girls in general are more careful of their clothes than boys, and may even be good about reporting tears and holes. Boys report these things, as a rule, only if these faults in clothing make them uncomfortable.

On taking clothes off at night, some Eight-year-olds drop them on the spot or just strew them around the room. An increasing number, however, do now throw clothes toward a chair, and a few may even put them *on* a chair. However, even those who are good about disposing of clothes at night seldom hang up outer garments during the day. Many can and do put dirty clothes in the hamper, at least if they are reminded to do so.

Most Eight-year-olds are quite interested in their clothes —color, style, even brand name. "I wanted Lees!" they may complain if Mother brings home some unfashionable or no-name brand. Style and color are important but even more important is what the "other kids" are wearing.

HEALTH AND SOMATIC COMPLAINTS

Eight's improved school attendance reflects not only his enjoyment of school but also his better health. If a girl or boy has a cold, it often lasts no more than two days. Even though temperatures may shoot up, the child tends to recover quickly. Occasionally an Eight-year-old may complain of a sore throat and then nothing more materializes. Hay fever and asthma may return after not being present for a year or so; there may also be an increase in the occurrence of ear infections, but most Eights have fewer gastrointestinal difficulties and fewer communicable diseases than they did earlier, and tend to recover more rapidly.

The Eight-year-old is in general much less fatigable than he was a year earlier. However, he may have a return of stomachaches if something upsets him, or he may have headaches from overexcitement. In fact, many Eights experience headaches, stomachaches, or a need to urinate when faced with any disagreeable task. As at Seven, there are now likely to be numerous eye complaints.

Eight-year-olds also tend to be accident-prone. In fact, accidents are a major cause of death at this age—chiefly accidents from automobiles, falls, and drowning. The Eight-year-old, like the Four-year-old, is out of bounds. He is out for action and is ready to try almost anything. He has lost the protective caution he had at Seven. He misjudges himself as being better than he really is. Eight is not really ready to take his bicycle out on the highway, as he usually wants to do. He is apt to get hit by a passing car. *It's crucial that parents provide the caution the child himself too often lacks.*

TENSIONAL OUTLETS

The tension outlets that parents of Eight-year-olds report are definitely fewer than those reported at Seven. Now the child's whole energy seems positively directed toward his social and gross motor activities, which are under better control than they were earlier. Thus children of this age seem to have less need than they did for tensional outlets.

At Eight the most common of these outlets is a need to urinate when taxed with something he does not like or is unequal to. Dish-wiping is sure to be interrupted almost immediately after it's begun by a trip to the bathroom. "Dishwater march," some mothers call it. A difficult school subject such as reading may produce a distended bladder in a very short time. This reaction may be thought of as "internal perspiration," emotionally induced. It is not just an alibi, as shown by the copiousness of the ensuing secretion. Intense laughter may also produce an involuntary release of urine.

A continuation of thumb-sucking in a small number of both boys and girls may prove discouraging to some parents. If the child did suck his thumb at Six he often tried to hide it from the adult; any children who were still sucking at Seven were at least trying to give it up. Eight may be a bit blatant about the whole thing, confessing no shame or embarrassment. Sucking tends to occur when children are reading, watching television, going to sleep.

Most will now work with their mothers in an effort to reduce this behavior. The thought of some desired object, such as a bike or watch, may do the trick. Others will wear a glove or accept the application of some nasty-tasting liquid. Children may even devise their own ways of giving up thumb-sucking.

At home, tensional outlets may be very diffuse. Any of the earlier patterns may appear: eye-blinking, nail-biting, picking at a mosquito bite, eye-rubbing, muttering, loud breathing. Some cry with fatigue. Many make faces when given an unwelcome command.

At school, any or all patterns of overflow common to Five- to Seven-year-olds may be seen, and often many different ones occur in a child during a single situation. Children may grimace, scowl, raise eyebrows, roll their eyes, hum, smack their lips, protrude their tongue. Leg-jiggling may be prominent, though some can control this by pressing their feet against the furniture or crossing their knees. Some express tension by fiddling with gadgets, on or in their desks.

chapter four
SELF AND SEX

SELF

At Seven the ego is strong but self-involved. At Eight the ego is trying to fit into the environment and is often having a hard time of it. The typical Seven builds up his sense of self by frequently withdrawing from the outside world. Now at Eight, the child takes that self out and tries it against the world. Eights seem almost unable to stay out of contact with any aspect of the world. Their boasting and alibiing probably both result from this effort to fit into their surroundings, and their difficulty in doing this to their own satisfaction.

The child of this age has become more of a person than he or she was at Seven. You don't have to make as many allowances for him as you did earlier. Rather you take him at face value, and he seems to respond to this. Your acceptance undoubtedly helps to build up and bolster his own sense of self. Many Eights seem to be coming out of the shyness and lack of self-confidence they exhibited just a year earlier.

At this time there is an increasing awareness of themselves as persons and of what they are like. Thus one Eight-year-old said to her mother, "I don't feel like myself" as she looked into a mirror on a train. Her mother commented that the girl had seen herself in a mirror before. The girl replied, "Yes, but this is the first time I've *really* seen myself."

As children read, watch television, attend movies, and widen their circle of friends and adults outside the family, they become increasingly aware of the similarities and differences in others' behavior and feelings. This extension of awareness of similarities, especially, tends to strengthen the child's identification with a social, economic, racial, religious, or national group.

Whatever adults may ultimately wish for in their children, at Eight the child definitely tends to prefer people who are like himself and to exclude those who are different. Family attitude, for most children, can help them understand the value of differences as well as likenesses.

Eight-year-olds love to be dramatic, to make a big deal out of occurrences that really are not all that big. They enjoy this dramatization even when they give the impression that they may be suffering: "This has got me crazy. Pretty soon I'll die of this."

On the other hand, they enjoy thinking about their own special qualities. One boy we know reported, on returning home, that he had developed a lot of *courage* at camp. This is a concept and evaluation rather beyond that of the average Seven-year-old.

At Seven, many of the child's difficulties seem to be within his own ego. At Eight, troubles occur as that ego meets the environment. Thus at Seven the child measures himself against his own demands. At Eight he measures himself against what he thinks are the demands of the adult.

Life isn't all roses at any age. One of the Eight-year-old's rather touching signs of vulnerability is his tendency to put down his own achievements and activities in order to get praise.

Another interesting aspect of the child's self at this age is his boldness of approach. Unless he is in a very bad mood, nothing is too difficult for the Eight-year-old, no task too formidable to undertake, no distance too great for him to cover. In fact, to the average child of this age, the new and difficult is an exciting challenge that he tends to meet with great zest.

Alas, he often overestimates his own ability to meet this challenge, and he does not always follow through in his activities. The burst of energy and enthusiasm with which he tackles each new task may be followed by failure, discouragement, and even tears if his failure is mentioned. If only his evaluativeness would spare him these painful failures more often!

For all his seeming brashness and bravado, the child of this age is much more sensitive than one might expect. He needs protection both from trying to do too much and from excessive self-criticism on those occasions when he does meet with failure. Thus when his good beginning is followed, as it sometimes will be, by a poor ending, parents should try to protect him from too great a feeling of failure. Plan with him toward a future time when he will carry through better or will set a more realistic goal for himself. The Eight-year-old has come a long way in his self-confidence, but he still has a long way to go.

Eight is extremely interested in and concerned about his own possessions—they are almost a part of his self. The child of this age likes to acquire and barter objects, likes to arrange them, gloats over them. He may or may not take good care of things but, regardless, likes and almost needs to have a good place of his own to keep things.

Not the least of Eight's property interest is money. This is an age at which many boys and girls can fairly be described as "money mad." This love of money unfortunately leads some to take household money in order to treat friends. However, many are interested enough in money to be willing to work to earn it. Most know how much they have, how much is due them, what they want to buy with it, and what things will cost. Some are quite good at saving up for expensive things and thus may be a little less likely than earlier to squander their money on frivolous items.

A strong part of any growing child's sense of self is his ethical sense. Eight, for all his expansiveness and exaggeration, is basically a rather reasonable person. On many occasions parents find that he can listen to reason and even can change his mind if he can be convinced that his own position is unreasonable. He can also make up his mind more easily than he could when younger.

Eights as a rule have a fairly clear idea of goodness and badness, right and wrong. The child is beginning to think more abstractly. Good and bad are no longer simply things that parents permit or forbid. Eight wants and means to be good, and tries hard to live up to his own standards and to what he thinks are the adult's standards.

Most Eight-year-olds are fairly good about taking the blame if they have done wrong. They may excuse their misdeed: "Do you blame me?" "Could I help it?" or they may deny their guilt but not blame somebody else as they might have done earlier. They may even act so maturely as to admit their guilt and promise that they will "never do it again."

Truthfulness may not be the Eight-year-old's strong point. His natural expansiveness tends to lead to boasting, exaggeration, and the telling of tall tales, even as at the somewhat similar age of Four. However, Eights can distinguish fact from fantasy and can usually—though not always—be counted on to tell the truth about things that really matter.

Eight is in general moving toward the acquisition of a reasonably good ethical sense, but in some respects, admittedly, he still has rather a long way to go.

SEX

As Dr. Gesell once remarked, rather poetically, "Though boys and girls participate as equals in school and recreational activities, and share many interests, they are also becoming vividly aware of distinctions that separate them. Their *expansive* trends may lead to experimentations, homosexual and heterosexual. Their divisive trends lead to withdrawal and to self-conscious unwillingness to touch each other even in ordinary play. The expansive trends also lead to new curiosities. There is an almost universal interest in babies. There are growing questionings about the origin of life, procreation and marriage."[5]

Though for the most part girls do seem to prefer to play with other girls, and boys with boys, a certain romantic note is creeping into the lives of both boys and girls. Boys recognize a pretty girl; girls chase handsome boys, much to the boys' delight.

A boy may ask his mother, "Is Bobby Blake handsome? The girls chase him. They're beginning to chase me too sometimes." Another boy, according to his mother, "is suffused with pleasure" when his girlfriend's name is mentioned, though he doesn't want to be teased about her. Some children of both sexes write notes to each other.

Having a girl (or boy) friend does not as a rule mean that the two children actually "go out" together, though they may indeed play together, at school or in informal neighborhood play. And there may be a certain amount of sex play, of an exploratory or exhibitionistic sort. Many boys are beginning to enjoy dirty jokes and smutty talk. There is a certain amount of interest in peeping, provocative giggling, whispering, or spelling out elimination or sex words. Thus one boy describes to his mother the word "rich," which he says *he* spells with a *b.* His mother told him her feelings about this and he desisted.

Most at Eight show a warm and loving interest in babies.

If they have not already been asked, and been told, about this at Seven or earlier, they are much interested in where babies come from, how they get out of the mother, and, of course, how they got into the mother in the first place. Whereas at Seven most were satisfied with the idea that two "seeds," one from each parent, got together, by now many are ready to be told about the father's part in the whole process. Some parents do feel embarrassed about answering these questions. It may be comforting to know that most children do not ask for answers beyond the point where they are ready to accept them.

Girls, as a rule, ask more questions about intercourse than boys do. Girls, too, if they have not already been told, tend now to be interested in the question of menstruation.

As to the child's own sexuality, this obviously is an important part of his sense of self. Although some individuals at any age express behavior more characteristic of the opposite sex, in our opinion in the majority of cases boys behave in what we traditionally think of as a "masculine" manner, girls in a "feminine" manner.

Nowadays some feminists insist that there are no innate sexual differences and that boys and girls would behave just alike if we treated them alike. Common sense, and most parents' observations, as well as our own, tell us that the two sexes tend to be worlds apart in their behavior. An occasional mother will tell you that she finds boys easier to raise than girls. The majority, however, say just the opposite. Most mothers we know of tell us that their boys were more difficult to raise than their girls, from infancy on.

Two recent reports on the matter confirm our own observations. One is by Pitcher and Schultz, who conclude their interesting and scholarly study of nursery-school boys and girls as follows:

Children learn narrow sex role concepts which conform in general to their culture's stereotyped belief system. Through their play behavior, children steadily incorporate the gender role initiated by their biology, demanded by their psyche, understood by their mind and supported by their culture. Human beings have characteristics which no society has created and to which all societies must respond. Young children acquire a sexual body from their genes, and they develop gender concepts from interaction with the environment. Both are formative influences in the child's becoming a male or female human being.[6]

Sara Bonnet Stein, in her extremely interesting book *Girls and Boys: The Limits of Non-sexist Child Rearing,* gives her reasons for the failure of those parents who have tried to make their boys and girls alike by what is called "nonsexist child-rearing." Her position is that the basic, genetic differences between the sexes are so central and so strong that even baby boys and baby girls impose their gender on their parents. Throughout toddlerhood and childhood, children continue to assert their gender. Her conclusion is that

We will have to remember that males and females may do the same things—fondle a baby, march for a cause, bring home a paycheck—but they must be free to experience and express these identical endeavours in their own unique ways.

This lesson we must learn from our children. They work hard to understand their gender clearly, to express it fearlessly, and in their own ways, to accept its constraints and to love its freedoms. Only by supporting their effort can we give our girls and boys the strength, the commitment, and the creativity to forge their own futures as women and men.[7]

Thus, at Eight as at other ages, on the whole girls and boys are extremely different from each other in their behavior and in their conceptions of themselves, however alike they may be in some respects.

chapter five
GENERAL INTERESTS AND ABILITIES

PLAY PREFERENCES AND ABILITIES

In General: The typical Eight-year-old does not like to play alone. He wants not only to have other people to share his play but wants their complete time and attention as well.

Action is the keynote to Eight's play activity. Even his drawings are full of action—airplanes and tanks are drawn in battle scene, or a person is shown piloting airplanes and maneuvering tanks. Boys put their tools to helpful household use by inserting hooks or screwing in loose doorknobs, though admittedly skill in using tools often does not keep pace with the child's ambitions. He is likely to start more than he can finish.

Girls mix up cooking ingredients to make cookies and cakes. Boys mix up the contents of their chemistry sets to produce new colors and smells, or to make what they call their "magic potions."

Eight loves to dramatize—accidents, fights, and car chases. Both girls and boys impersonate characters in movies they have seen or books they have read. Girls, especially, love to dress up and put on "shows." They may even charge admission. Boys love magic tricks as well as acting.

Though there are many kinds of play that they enjoy in

common, particularly an interest in working home computers, in general the kinds of play enjoyed by the two sexes is definitely diverging. Dolls are big with girls. Boys especially like to use tools and to play with their chemistry sets or models or electric trains.

Paper dolls provide a good vehicle for a girl's dramatic urge. They also serve as an outlet for Eight's powerful urge to collect. Paper dolls and their dresses can be collected in quantity. And Eight likes to classify, arrange, and organize them.

A love of "real" dolls can still be very strong as well. Girls will, for instance, put their dolls through the whole routine of a day—but now it can be more at the child's own personal pace rather than having the doll's whole day fly by in a few minutes, as earlier. Or a girl may speak for her doll—telling some adult that the doll doesn't like the adult. Then as time proceeds, she may say that the doll is *getting to* like the person. Cabbage Patch dolls were for a brief time popular with many, though this turned out to be a passing fad. To some extent, and briefly, they supplanted the Barbie and Ken dolls so popular earlier. (Though the manufacturers of Barbie and Ken have successfully updated their product and now offer an *Island Fun* Barbie.)

Doll play, in which many girls like to have their mother take part, often consists of activities not particularly interesting to the adult. It involves much conversation, on the part of the girl herself or the girl representing her doll. And she wants Mother to take part fully in these sometimes seemingly endless conversations.

Boys even more than girls love collecting, and they will collect—almost anything. They are interested not only in quantity, however. Now many are becoming interested in quality and in rudimentary classification. They are also interested in bartering. As they barter they usually exchange like for like—comic books for comic books (or with girls, doll clothes for doll clothes). However, their evaluation is not always too good and the bargain is apt to be very bad on one side or the other. (This tends to distress the parent more than it does the child.)

Gross motor activity is characteristic of the Eight-year-old group play but the child may need some restraint. Children of this age too readily go out of bounds. When a group of Eights are left to their own devices, they often revert to "animal spirits"—wild running, jumping, chasing, wrestling, tree climbing. They are, however, capable of organizing simple war games or a game of hide-and-seek. And for all their abandon they usually respond well to supervised control.

Eight enjoys the different sports in season. He swims in summer, skis and skates in the winter. He likes such team sports as baseball and soccer. Actually, though baseball may in some communities be the more popular, it may bring more pain than pleasure to some of the players if the coach is highly competitive and uses only the best players. Soccer offers more opportunity for all the players, even the less skilled, to take part.

Interest in table games—especially cards, Parcheesi, checkers, Monopoly—reaches an almost passionate height. Although some Eights can lose with fair grace, even at this age it's not always true and a good deal of bickering and some accusations of cheating occur.

Boys make airplane models, draw airplanes, indulge in imaginative airplane play. Interest in Legos and mechanical toys continues to be strong. Electric trains, chemistry sets, small movie projectors with real film, are enjoyed by many.

One Eight-year-old of our acquaintance, when asked what he liked to do for fun, provided this rather comprehensive list: "Play soccer, watch TV, make model airplanes, play war, fight with my brothers, play baseball, make monsters out of paper (draw them and cut them out), play Dungeons and Dragons (you make guns and bows and arrows and swords out of sticks and stuff), read books, play with

my friends, play checkers, play 'ungame,' go swimming, go camping (I like to chop down trees, just little ones, with my little saw/shovel/nail puller/ screwdriver)."

Reading and Writing: Eight-year-olds often like to read for fun, and those Eights who are reasonably good readers now read of their own accord, without prompting. They may enjoy the classics of childhood or books of jokes, rhymes, riddles. Children of this age like to explore new types of books in their reading. Thus they like the unfamiliar ground of a mystery, the expansiveness offered by books of travel, books set in faraway places and times. They like books about other children, animals, fairies, the elements, adventure. They are very quick to express scorn for a book or story that they consider too young for them.

Comic books are still favorites, though perhaps not as much so as they used to be before television viewing became so prevalent. Eights also like to look at pictorial magazines and can spend hours poring over catalogs. They plan to send away for things, though actually they may never get around to doing this.

Writing can also be used for entertainment. Some of the more literary among them are already writing little stories or poems, or even writing letters to friends. And they love to get mail of their own.

Music, Radio, Television, and Movies: The initial Seven-year-old flare of interest in taking music lessons may have died out, though those for whom music is really very probably continue to be enthusiastic. Practicing should not be forced, and it may be wise to interrupt lessons for a while if the child's initial interest does not hold up. However, some whose interest may be waning slightly will practice if somebody sits with them.

Television has now become such an important part of the child's life that he will neglect play for it. This is the one activity he enjoys alone, though most are pleased if someone wants to watch with them. Eights are beginning to choose their own programs more selectively than earlier and will even refer to *TV Guide* or the newspaper listings. They watch the same programs each day or week and know just when they come on. While they may still cling to cartoons and special children's programs, many are branching out into sitcoms and quiz shows. Among current favorites are *Thundercats, Transformers, Danger Mouse, Wuzzles, Muppet Babies and Monsters, Charlie Brown,* and *Scoobie Doo.* Most dislike the news.

Many Eights would watch as long as they are permitted to, though the amount of viewing varies tremendously, largely depending on what parents will allow. Many critics of television bemoan the fact that American children spend as much (or more) time watching television as they spend in school. For those who spend long, unsupervised hours of weekend viewing, this may be true. In a small group of Eight-year-olds whom we surveyed, weekend viewing ranged from one to twelve hours on Saturday and on Sunday, though the weekend *average* for girls was only five hours on Saturday and four on Sunday; for boys the average was six hours on Saturdays and four on Sundays. Weekday viewing ranged from one to eight hours for girls with an average of three and a half hours. For boys the range was only half an hour to seven hours a day, with an average of four hours. These figures compare fairly well to figures we obtained by questioning over 1,000 Ten-year-olds. At that age girls reported an average weekly viewing time of twenty hours; boys of twenty-five.

Most Eight-year-olds go to the movies occasionally but many seem quite content to stay at home and watch rented movies on the family VCR. If they do go out to the movies, most like animal films or mysteries and hate romantic movies. If things on the screen become too much for them, some cry, some look away, some leave for the lobby.

THE CHILD'S BODY IN ACTION

Posture is now more symmetric than earlier. In writing, postures tend to be somewhat variable. Though the head may be tilted to one side or the other, it is usually straight. Some have the nondominant arm at their side, but others place it on the tabletop. Some do lean forward but the upright position is usually preferred, or at least attempted.

The bodily movements of an Eight-year-old are fluid and often graceful and poised. The child's walk is free. He is aware of his own posture and remembers to sit up straight on occasion. In fact, he is ready to criticize others who don't. He likes to dramatize and express himself in a variety of postures and gestures.

The Eight-year-old tends to be very active physically, always on the go. He runs, jumps, chases, wrestles. Hide-and-seek is a favorite pastime, but he is also ready for more organized sports such as soccer and baseball. Eights are now good spectators as well as performers.

Courage and daring are characteristics of Eight. If he climbs trees or walks a plank, he steels himself. He may verbalize his fear and may need encouragement, but often accomplishes what he sets out to do.

There is a new enjoyment in skating, jumping rope, or swimming, and the child is more receptive to learning new techniques. But he is so spontaneous that he frequently goes his own way regardless, after he has tried it your way.

Large muscle control is now well established. Small muscles develop noticeably during this year. Children become interested in sewing, weaving, finer paper cutting, intricate woodwork. However, there is apt to be a gap between things they want to do with their hands and what they actually can accomplish. Often they feel thwarted if things don't turn out the way they had planned.

There is an increase of speed and smoothness in fine motor performance and in eye-hand coordination. Approach and grasp are rapid, smooth, and even graceful; release is with sure abandon. The child holds a pencil, brush, tools, less tensely than he did earlier.

Eight can change his posture adaptively. He bends forward, then sits upright so that as he works on a task his head is at various distances from his working point. There is more symmetry than at Seven, and he frequently rests on both elbows or extends both arms out on the table in front of him.

Eight can look before he acts, but he also likes to do things speedily, so the preliminary pause before he attacks a task is usually not too long.

VISION

Eight is an expansive age, and the Eight-year-old may be thought of as peripherally oriented. Along with this new orientation there is an increased flexibility in the use of the eyes. The child can shift from near to far with greater ease, though he may still have difficulty in shifting back, from far to near. Though most do a better job of copying from the board than they did at Seven, they may lose things at near point if they are following them, as in watching a ball thrown at them. But in any visual adjustment, they tend to be less intense and more speedy than they were a year earlier.

The child of this age is more distracted (as earlier at age Six) by things seen in peripheral vision. Thus in school he may be much more interested in looking out of the window than in looking at a book.

Eight expands and tries to include more and more visually, and thus is likely to become confused. Bicycle accidents and getting hit with thrown balls occur partly because he doesn't know where he is visually. However, he now has an improved view of spatial relationships. He recognizes, also, that another person can view a scene differently from the way he sees it, and perspective is appearing in his drawings.

The child of this age does not touch what he sees as much as he did formerly. Those who still have to touch everything may be having trouble in visual orientation. They need to confirm with their hands what they see with their eyes.

Eights may object to wearing glasses. For those who do, it would be wise to check with the child's vision specialist to see if the child really must wear glasses during all of his waking hours. He may not have to.

chapter six
THE CHILD'S MIND

Practically everything a child does gives us clues as to how his or her mind is working. However, in this chapter we restrict ourselves to the kinds of behavior that people customarily think of as expressions of the mind in action. Thus we write about the child's sense of time and space; ability in reading, writing, and arithmetic; level of thinking; and ability to express himself through verbal language. And finally, we discuss his concepts of death, deity, and Santa Claus.

TIME

The child of Eight is becoming more responsible than he was earlier with regard to time. His increased speed in action makes him less vulnerable to the demands of time, as he accomplishes things more quickly than when he was Seven. (It also makes him impatient to be older, to grow up.)

The child can now be expected to arrive at school on time, and without all the fuss and anxiety he exhibited at Seven. He likes to know where he is in time; for instance, he likes to consult the bulletin board about the school schedule.

Eight is extremely aware of punctuality, of what time he should be at different places. He can tell time, but may still depend on his parents to tell him that it is bedtime. Getting to school on time is important and he can usually do it; going to bed is much less important and he may need quite a bit of reminding. He is interested in his TV programs and so can usually tune in on them in plenty of time.

The child of this age can also tell what day of the month it is and what year it is. He can also name the months of the year.

Eight is very much interested in times far past. He likes to hear and read about things that happened in the early days of this country, though he is not always too clear about when things occurred. Thus he is not clear as to whether George Washington is mentioned in the Bible. An interest in Indians and Pilgrims may now take the place of his earlier interest in policemen and firemen.

SPACE

Personal space is expanding for the Eight-year-old. He can now travel by himself on a bus on a familiar or prearranged route. He enjoys moving about the neighborhood and sometimes goes out of bounds in trespassing on neighboring property.

Eight, with his interest in space, is usually very enthusiastic about geography. He likes to draw maps, likes to learn about the different cities and states. He is interested in what is happening in foreign countries as well as in his own.

Though some Eight-year-olds tend to be reasonably well oriented in space, this is not true of all. Some children have a very poor idea of spatial relationships, even in familiar surroundings. Some researchers, we among them, consider that it is the right-brained, left-handed children who do best in physical space, or in putting together puzzles that require a good understanding of spatial relationships; the left-brained, right-handed children are more spatially inept. Whether this is the case or not, it certainly is true that some children are much better than others both in knowing what time it is and where they are.

READING, WRITING, AND ARITHMETIC

Reading: Most Eights enjoy reading. They can tackle new words through context or by division into syllables, initial consonants, or prefixes or suffixes. They are more skillful than they were a year earlier and only occasionally make the errors so common at Seven. There is much less trouble with vowels. The child now may omit unimportant words or reverse word order in a phrase, but usually maintains the meaning. The mechanisms of reading, and reading for meaning, are now in better balance. The child also has a more uniform speed than earlier and can stop and talk about a story and then pick up reading again. Many prefer silent reading and read more rapidly when they read silently.

According to reading specialist Jeanne Chall, as they learn to read, children go through rather definite stages of reading ability. In the first stage, characteristic of Sixes and Sevens, the child is merely decoding. By the second stage, usually reached by Seven to Eight, he reaches the stage of "confirmation, fluency, unglueing from print." This stage consolidates what was learned in Stage 1. In the Seven- to Eight-year-old stage, reading is not yet for gaining new information so much as for confirming what is already known to the reader. The reader can take advantage of what is said in the story or book, matching it to his own knowledge. But children are still learning to read. They have not quite reached the stage at which they read to learn new information.

If a boy or girl is still having trouble with reading, this is a good time for someone to step in. First, the parents should check to be sure that the problem is not simply that the

child is a good reader but is reading at a younger level. He may be reading like a Seven-year-old rather than an Eight. If other behaviors also are at a Seven-year-old level, the problem may be simply that he is overplaced in school. Or there may be a perceptual problem. However, if neither of these things is true, then this may be a good age for Mother to step in.

As mentioned, most Eights love to be with their mother, sharing with her, working with her, playing with her, talking with her. Reading exercises, even if they are considered a chore (as they will be by many children), will as a rule nevertheless be accepted if they mean more time alone with Mother and if they mean that the child will have her exclusive attention.

As Eight likes to bargain, the bargain could be that after a certain amount of time spent on reading exercises, Mother and child will spend an equal amount of time doing something (probably playing games) the child will enjoy.

Of course, not all reading problems can be solved so easily. Admittedly there are some boys and girls (probably more boys than girls) who are going to need help from a reading specialist or teachers. Then it is the parent's, as well as the school's, responsibility to see that this help is provided.

Writing: Writing is less laborious than earlier and there is more uniformity in slant and alignment as well as in spacing of words and sentences. There may be an occasional rare reversal or a substitution of a capital for a small letter in manuscript writing. There is considerable variation from child to child. Many now write cursively instead of printing. Some tend to write fairly large and rather "squarely" with a slight slant. Some write medium size and evenly though still straight without a slant. If writing is becoming smaller, then capitals and looped letters tend to be disproportionately tall.

Most Eights write both names with good spacing and correct use of capital and small letters, though there is still a discrepancy in size between capital and small letters and great variation from child to child in size and style of writing.

Eight *tries* to write neatly. "I'm doing my best writing." "Is this neat?" Doodling or drawing in notebooks or on scrap paper is a favorite activity. He is now more aware of body proportions in his drawing of human figures, and he particularly likes to draw people in action. He is beginning to draw in perspective.

Arithmetic: As for arithmetic, Eight likes variety. He likes oral or written arithmetic; he likes to use the chalkboard but also to work in his workbook. He is partial to the new tables he is learning and likes to shift from one process

to another. But he's unpredictable, one day he may say he doesn't like arithmetic and the next day he will tell you that it is easy.

Most can count by threes to thirty and by fours to forty. They rarely make an error in writing numbers through twenty or higher. In addition, they know many combinations by heart. Any errors are mostly plus or minus one. The same goes for subtraction. Learning to add and subtract one- to three-digit numbers requires borrowing and carrying, which most have mastered. Most can multiply through both the four and the six tables. They also can use the simple facts of short division. Most can use fractions of one-half and one-quarter.

Many confuse their process, for instance, switch to adding when they are supposed to be multiplying.

THINKING AND LANGUAGE

Probably the person who has written the most about the stages through which the child's thinking develops is the famous Swiss philosopher Jean Piaget. As his own writing is rather hard to understand, most of us rely on books that explain what Piaget really meant in our efforts to interpret his work. Thus explanations vary a bit, but most agree in labeling the Seven- to Eleven-year-old stage of thinking as *concrete operational,* or the beginning of abstraction.

When they reach this stage, children are less self-centered than earlier. They now recognize the views of others. They also see the ways objects are alike and different. They know, for instance, that the shape of a container does not affect the quantity it holds. (This is very important in Piaget's thinking, though in real life it actually does not come up too often.)

Both an Eight-year-old and a Five-year-old may intuitively sense that there is more water in a tall, thin cylinder than in a flat dish in which the water rested moments earlier. But the older child subdues the intuition with a recently acquired *rule* that states that the amount of water in a vessel must remain the same if the only change is the shape of the container holding it.

Eights also understand the idea of number. They can tell that ten marbles in a row are more than eight in a row even if the two rows are of the same length. Before this they would think the numbers were the *same* if the rows were of equal length.

The Eight-year-old can apply simple logic to arrive at a conclusion, can reason deductively, and now can classify. Also he is able to picture a series of actions, such as going on an errand and returning. Before this age he could not draw a map of where he would go. Following a familiar route (which children can do when younger) is different from visualizing it.

One big aspect of thinking at Eight is that the child is becoming less animistic (believing that natural phenomena and inanimate things have souls). Now he is growing aware of the impersonal forces of nature. He knows what makes a sailboat go. He can distinguish fundamental similarities and differences in objects.

On the whole, Eight has a certain power of intellectual rebound. He can be influenced to check up on his clues when he has jumped to a conclusion too quickly. But he does not want you to think for him—he wants only a hint that will help him to work things out for himself.

Contrary to our own position, which maintains, following Dr. Gesell's thinking, that "Mind manifests itself in virtually everything the person does," Piaget discusses mind chiefly in terms of verbally expressed thinking. According to the Gesell position, the child's mind directs and controls virtually everything he or she does. Thus nearly everything we describe in this book represents some aspect of the mind in action.

However, sticking to the Piaget approach for the moment, we'll discuss further the *language* of the Eight-year-old as we have observed it. To begin with, as part of his customarily expansive nature, the typical Eight-year-old talks a lot. He uses language fluently, expansively. He exaggerates, boasts, tells tall tales. Thus he can tell you an impressive and very lifelike (though untrue) story about hitting a home run in a baseball game.

He speaks not only in ordinary English (or whatever his native language may be) but may now be interested in code language, such as Pig Latin or Double Dutch, or may enjoy the use of secret passwords. There is also considerable use of slang and of some profanity, though if family and school backgrounds are favorable, there also tends to be good pronunciation and reasonably good use of grammar.

For all that he is not yet completely truthful, Eight as a rule can differentiate very clearly between fantasy and reality. And though he tends to be much interested in magicians and their tricks—may even like to perform simple card tricks himself—he shows less belief in magic than he did just earlier.

Intellectually, Eight can cite not only similarities and differences between simple objects, he also begins to understand cause-and-effect relationships.

There tends to be considerable social use of the telephone at Eight. Language is really coming into its own.

DEATH, DEITY, AND SANTA CLAUS

As with other intellectual concepts, Eights tend to show a lively interest in death. In his more positive vein, the child of this age has moved from what some may have considered a moderately morbid interest in graves and funerals, to an interest in what happens after death. Eights show a rather positive enthusiasm about the notion of one day going to heaven and accept the notion that probably the soul and not the body goes there.

Those of a religious bent may conceive of death as an immediate act of God, as the result of some disease, or as resulting from a disease that in turn may be a punishment from God. Most, however, do not dwell on any of these possibilities.

Eights verbalize much less than Sevens that they wish they were dead. In fact, many seem quite calm about the eventuality of death, seemingly accepting the fact that all people, including themselves, do die. As one little boy replied when asked how he felt about dying, "It's all right with me."

Though some Sevens do express a certain skepticism

about the reality of God, Eights in general do accept the idea—"I believe what they tell me"—and express little concern or even interest one way or the other. Believers believe, and children whose families are not religious make relatively little comment. Some, believers or not, do like to read Bible stories.

Eight-year-olds are at the far edge of believing in Santa Claus. Probably most do not believe, though some still do leave out milk and cookies just in case he should arrive. One Eight of our acquaintance, who had expressed marked (though somewhat reluctant) skepticism on Christmas Eve, shouted out with great relief, "He came! He came!" when he saw the food gone and the stockings hung by the fireplace. Some, however, seem to be moving very comfortably into a realm where they are beginning to accept the notion of "spirit of Christmas" or "spirit of giving" over the more corporeal Santa. Eight-year-olds, believing in Santa or not, like to make a good long list of things they want for Christmas, but most are now mature enough to accept a parent's explanation that they will probably not receive everything on the list.

ETHICAL BEHAVIOR

The area of ethical behavior, or morals, is one of the many areas where the mind at work can be seen most clearly. Truthfulness, or the lack of it, concerns most parents. Fortunately, most Eights are relatively truthful about matters they consider really important. Their natural expansiveness may, however, lead to a little boasting and exaggeration, and some do tell rather tall tales about their alleged accomplishments. But most can differentiate fact from fantasy, and even when telling a tall tale an Eight may eye the adult carefully to see if what he is saying is being believed.

Your typical Eight-year-old wants to be good. He is now

more aware of the two opposing forces of good and bad and may see goodness and badness as more than merely what his parents permit or forbid. He is definitely beginning to think in terms of right and wrong, not just in terms of good and bad. He may be so concerned about them as absolutes that his parents will have to help him to think relatively in order to make allowances for the "badness" of a younger sibling.

Eight-year-olds do not necessarily obey instructions or requests immediately. They may argue and find excuses, but in the end usually obey, perhaps with the comment, "If you insist."

One Eight-year-old of our acquaintance asked his mother if she would do him a favor. She agreed. The favor was: "When you call me for dinner, instead of saying 'Johnny, come to dinner!' would you just say, 'Chief Rain-in-the Face, wahoo, wahoo, wahoo.' "

"I think I could do that," Johnny's mother said with a smile, and for about a week she announced dinner in the manner he had requested. At the end of that time, her son told her, "I think it would be okay if you just called me in the regular way."

Eight-year-olds do try to do right, at least most of the time, and they love praise for what they have done. If criticized they may either break into tears or may, at the opposite extreme, merely shrug it off with "Who cares?"

Although Eight is becoming more responsible for his acts and is willing to accept the consequences, his first and usual impulse still may be to blame others. He is apt to insist that somebody else "started" the trouble. He especially alibies about being late: "I didn't know what time it was," or "My friends wouldn't let me go." However, if guilt is clearly apparent, most will apologize and/or promise not to do (whatever it was) again.

The same child who at Six dictated to her mother a list of "Things to Do and Things Not to Do," and at Seven a list of things involved in "Thinking About Myself" and "Thinking About Others," now at Eight asked her mother to write down her idea of things that were "Right and Wrong." It is interesting to note that this is a single-column list. Right and Wrong are to some extent brought together into a single standard of conduct and are no longer separated into bipolar opposition. The list follows:

RIGHT AND WRONG

1. It's not my fault that they call me a "bad sport" when I want to play a different game after I've played one for a long time. I can't help it if there aren't enough people to start another game. Finally I get up enough strength to play some more. And finally they change the game.

2. Question of getting to school on time! How can I tell the exact time I've got to get up and the exact time to eat breakfast so I can get to school on time? I can't help it if I'm late. It's not my fault. Probably all my guesses about time are all wrong.

3. When some of the people start up a fight, it's not my fault if I want to try and stop the fight even though Miss D. tells us to keep away from fights because the other teachers would think we'd started them. Even if we try to explain to the teachers, they think we did start the fight and were just trying to get away from being punished.

4. Something hard comes up and I'm trying to do it. I don't think it's fair for other people to come along and call me a "sissy" because I can't do it very well. (Some of these things haven't happened yet but they might.)

5. In the coatroom, even though you're not supposed to talk, I can't help it sometimes because other people ask me questions and tempt me to answer them. Do you blame me?

6. Running in the halls going out to recess. I can't help

running in the halls because I'm so eager to go out to shout and play.

7. I think I ought to have a little more freedom, more freedom about deciding things—like getting up early in the morning (I used to plan to, then I'd be too tired when I woke up).

8. I think I should have rewards for being good, like candy and books I like very much. But I won't always have to be rewarded. Maybe when I'm about Nine and a half or Ten I don't think I'll have to be rewarded for being good. Then I'll just be good naturally.

9. If it's a sensible reason and something I can do quite easily and something I feel I can do and want to do, and don't have to force myself to do, then I should obey.

10. I think I should do something about getting up in the morning. I ought to be able to choose sensible clothes. And if I don't, it serves me right to have to take them off unless they are sensible.

11. You shouldn't just force me to do things. I will do them if they are sensible.

12. On the playground it's not my fault if I want to slide on a wonderful sliding place in the back of the school and I'd forgotten at that minute that I wasn't supposed to play in the back. (Oh, it was neat ice, and there was a little bump at the end.)

RESPONSE TO REASON; HONESTY; PROPERTY SENSE

Though Eights may be quite insistent about having their own way, most are in general able to listen to reason, and most can make up their minds about things fairly easily.

As far as honesty is concerned, most are relatively honest though some, as earlier, take household money in order to "treat" their friends. And taking money may not be related merely to buying things for friends. Money is now extremely meaningful to the child in terms of what it will buy, and if he thinks his needs are not provided for, he may take money, as from his mother's pocketbook. Some, more honest, like to earn the money they want and need. There is less squandering of money on trifles than earlier, more saving up for big things.

Entirely honest or not, most have a rather strong sense of property, a great interest in possessions. They hoard, arrange, and gloat over their own possessions. It is important to the child to have a place of his own to keep his things. Some take good care of their things, but in general it is fair to say that most Eights tend to be quite careless. Certainly one can count on their rooms being messy.

chapter seven
SCHOOL

BEHAVIOR IN GENERAL

Most Eight-year-olds love school and are unhappy if they have to stay at home, particularly if it means missing some special event. Even though the child may not be doing well in his work or getting along with his teacher, Eight's attitude tends to be one of real enthusiasm for school. The ambiguity he may have felt at Seven is gone. The child tires less easily now; his attendance record is usually good and there tend to be fewer absences due to illness. If out for a day or two, the child wants his schoolwork sent home so that he will not get behind.

Some Eights, especially boys, may still have difficulty in getting ready for school, and on time. It is often hard to motivate them at home, as they are no longer as fearful of being late as they were at Seven. However, they may be motivated by a new responsibility they've been given in school that challenges them. Getting to school on time is now up to the school as well as the family, and buses are provided in most communities. Of course, the child is still responsible for reaching the bus on time.

There is usually more interplay between home and school than there was earlier. Eight likes to take things home and often likes to report at home about all the terrible, or wonderful, things that went on in school, much more so than at Seven.

Children at this age are strongly aware of the performance ability of the other children. Some people think it is the competitive attitude of our American schools that makes children compete. Actually, it is often just their own temperament. They like to beat their own record or somebody else's. But most are surprisingly tolerant of other children who may not be very good at arithmetic, or reading, or some other subject. On the other hand, they are so eager to move ahead that it is hard for them to wait for a slow child.

Eight, with his increasing visual ability, can now copy things from the chalkboard, shifting his eyes more easily from board to desk than he was able to at Seven. And he likes to write on the board. However, this may make a problem for those certain children who are not yet fully up to board copying. Also, third grade is much harder for many than second, as now the teacher gives fewer instructions. Often children are supposed to discover from the board what they are expected to do, and the less mature ones may not be fully up to this.

Most Eights like their teacher, but they especially love to catch her in a mistake. This is particularly so if she has a good sense of humor and will admit that she too is human. But Eight does not depend on his teacher as much as he did earlier. There is at Eight a new spirit of self-reliance, as there needs to be. To some extent the children control each other's activity. They are very capable of evaluating the performance of others: "He's not very good at arithmetic."

For the most part, Eight-year-olds tend to keep themselves fairly busy at school. There is less daydreaming or goofing off than there was at younger ages. However, Eights are gregarious and like to do quite a lot of talking to neighbors. If this communication is not excessive, it probably should be permitted. It is hard for the child of this age to wait if he has something to say. Eight-year-olds are not only fully aware of other children's strong points and weak ones but also of their own, and they like to discuss both. In school, as elsewhere, Eight loves to be praised, by teacher and by classmates.

Eight-year-olds are especially oriented to their own group, room, and teacher. The group is important to them, as is their place in the group. Thus if the child of this age can, for the most part, have a single teacher rather than many different ones during the course of a day, his life will be smoother. He likes his group and does not want to be separated from it.

Most are coming along reasonably well with their school subjects. This progress is described in some detail in Chapter 6. However, briefly, it can be noted that writing is now less laborious and there is more uniformity in slant and alignment as well as in spacing of words and sentences. There may be an occasional reversal or a substitution of a capital for a small letter.

Eight, in arithmetic as in other areas, likes variety. He likes oral and written arithmetic; likes to use the chalkboard and to work at his desk. Most are partial to the new tables they are learning. They like to shift from one process to another. Some like to take their workbook home to catch up, and may even go beyond a given assignment.

And, expansive Eight is truly interested in geography. Somehow he grasps a sense of the whole country, the whole continent, the whole world, and even the whole universe.

EVERY CHILD IN THE RIGHT GRADE

Let's say your Eight-year-old boy or girl is *not* doing well in the third grade. Perhaps somebody has even labelled him or her as learning disabled. Some children, though many fewer than are so categorized, may indeed be learning disabled. There are many reasons for school failure.

But the chief reason we have observed, the one we have

observed most often, is simple overplacement. Many perfectly bright little boys and girls, who have no serious intellectual or perceptual problems, who have supportive homes, who really do try their very best, fail in school simply because they started too soon, whatever their chronological age, and thus are in a grade for which they are not ready.

All too many parents and administrators assume that just because a child is five years of age, he or she is behaving like a full Five and thus is ready for kindergarten. However, individual differences in growth rate abound, and many perfectly bright and normal children are not Five in their behavior, despite their chronological age. And thus they should wait an extra year to begin school.

Our own recommendation, and a policy that is now in actual practice in hundreds of schools around the country, is that all children start school, and be subsequently promoted, on the basis of their behavior age, not their age in years. Certain tests (among them our own) can be given to all school beginners (and to older children when any question about their grade placement comes up) to determine whether they are ready to start school or, when the time comes, to be promoted.

We list here signs and signals, developed by a teaching principal, that a child might be overplaced, or unready. Any parent or teacher can check these signs. (It is, of course, important to keep in mind that all children display some of these signs at times, and that some signs and signals transcend grade levels. That is, they could occur at any age.)

THIRD GRADE: SIGNS AND SIGNALS OF STRESS [8]

At Home:
1. Complains about the volume of schoolwork.
2. Picks on siblings.

3. Develops a psychosomatic illness—i.e., a stomach-ache, a headache, a sore leg, a limp, a temperature.

At School: A third-grader who is over his head may

1. Prefer to play with second-graders.
2. Dislike certain subjects. (Knows he's behind and doesn't know how to do the work.)
3. Find cursive writing extremely difficult; writes laboriously.
4. Be overwhelmed by the volume of work.
5. Be incapable of working independently.
6. Ask if she or he can visit second grade.
7. Frequently say, "My old teacher did it this way."
8. Find copying from the chalkboard extremely difficult.
9. Be unable to memorize the multiplication tables.
10. Habitually lose or destroy worksheets.
11. Find shifting from soft workbooks to hardcover textbooks very difficult.

In General: A third-grader who is under an excessive amount of stress may

1. Cherish toys and make them more important than is appropriate for his age.
2. Develop a nervous tic—a twitching eye, a nervous cough, twirling the hair, clearing the throat, etc.
3. Seem not to fit into his peer group.
4. Take out his frustrations on other children during play.
5. Be picked on or rejected by peers and called names: "dumb," "stupid," "airhead," etc.
6. Have a hard time learning to tell time, prefer wearing a digital watch.
7. Chew on pencils, buttons, hair, collars, or whatever is handy.

8. Find change threatening; have a hard time handling new situations.

EXPECTED RESPONSES TO GESELL BEHAVIOR (READINESS) TEST SITUATIONS

In addition to checking on home and classroom behaviors that may, of themselves, quite clearly indicate that any third-grader may indeed be overplaced, a suspicion that this may be the case can be confirmed by giving the child a battery of developmental (or readiness) tests.

Listed below are indications of the ways we would expect an Eight-year-old child, if up to his age and thus presumably ready for third-grade work, to respond to our Gesell Readiness Tests.

Paper and Pencil: Children of this age can, of course, write their names. About half write cursively. Size of letters is more consistent than it was, and capitals and smaller letters are used correctly. There are usually no reversals or substitutions. Last name is placed properly in relation to the first, with good spacing between.

Although writing or printing their entire address is not altogether easy, Eights are ready to tackle this task though most would prefer to write only their street address. There may be some trouble with spelling and/or punctuation. Even Eights who can write their name cursively may print their address. Most do not yet grasp the total concept of a name and address as it would be placed on a letter, but tend to string name and address out on one or two lines.

At this age, 54 percent of girls whom we tested and 46 percent of boys can write or print their street and number, city, and state. When we see an Eight-year-old struggle with cursive writing, with letters growing larger and lines drooping down, we might question as to whether third-graders should be required to write cursively.

Though most Seven-year-olds can name the day's date, it

is not until Eight that the majority can write, correctly, the month, day, and year. Eight is the second age at which the majority of boys and girls can write the numbers one to twenty, with even size and a relatively even base line.

Copying Geometric Forms: The forms that we at Gesell ask children to copy are the circle, cross, square, triangle, divided rectangle ▷◁, and diamond. At Seven and thus also at Eight nearly all children can copy all of these forms correctly, and they copy the circle from the top down and counterclockwise.

Most now use half a page to one page for all these figures. Arrangement in a horizontal row is normative in girls, not quite normative in boys (42 percent of boys do achieve this arrangement). Nearly half the girls (46 percent) make the forms of even size. Boys forms are very variable in size.

Completing the Incomplete Figure of a Man: The average number of parts now added is ten. (See Figure 3.) This includes most of the following: hair, eyes, pupils, ear, two or three parts at the neck, arm and fingers, leg and foot.

The arm for most is placed accurately (in the upper third of the body), points upward, and is either of the right length or too short. The three fingers may be shaped nicely. Leg placement and length are improving though the leg may be too straight and too short. The foot points in the correct direction and is usually of a good length.

Hair is very variable and has not as yet come into graduated lengths. The big thing here is the increasing expression in the eyes. Some eyes are oval or approaching an oval shape and have pupils. Ear shape is improving, and many Eights try to shape the ear correctly.

The majority of both sexes add three parts (neck, bow, and body line) at the neck area.

Response to the Munroe Visual Three: The Munroe Visual Three is a test in which sixteen figures (four on each of four cards) are to be reproduced from memory. The average Eight-year-old can reproduce eight or nine of these forms,

some from each card. Fifty percent or more respond correctly to figures 1 and 2 on Cards 1 and 2. Some other figures are remembered correctly, but these vary from child to child. The average number of forms reproduced correctly, from memory, is now 8.8 for girls, 8.9 for boys. Nearly all copy some figures from all four lines.

Understanding Right and Left and Parts of the Body: Fifty percent or more of Eight-year-olds can name eye, eyebrow, palm, elbow, thumb, index finger, middle finger (with help), and ring finger. They still cannot name their little finger. They know their own right and left hands (and have for some time), and nearly all can also identify the examiner's right hand, though their reasons for being able to do this are very varied.

Answers to Personal Questions: The Eight-year-old can, of course, tell his age and also the day and month of his birthday. He can also tell names and ages of siblings. In fact, the personal interview questions asked earlier are not particularly useful at this age, as they are too easy for most Eights.

Naming Animals for One Minute: Now as at every age

from Six on, the majority can name animals for one minute. The average number of animals named by girls is twelve; by boys, fourteen. Girls name chiefly domestic animals, especially dog; boys name chiefly zoo animals, especially lion.

Projective Techniques: One special way psychologists have of measuring a child's mind is through the use of what we call projective techniques. A projective technique is a kind of test to which there are no right or wrong responses. Rather, the child or adult projects his personality or way of thinking and experiencing onto what may be considered a rather fluid medium.

One of the best known of these techniques is the Rorschach Inkblot Test. In giving this test, we show the child a series of cards, on each of which is printed a more or less shapeless inkblot. Some of the blots are colored, some black and white. We ask the child to tell us what the blots look like to him. From what he says we believe we can tell a good deal about what he is like and what the world looks like to him.

Not only do different children see different things, but, in general, different kinds of things are seen at different ages. Thus the personality characteristics of any given age as well as the characteristics of the individual child seem to make themselves evident in the individual's response to the inkblots.

The typical Rorschach response at Eight seems to confirm what we have observed in more homespun ways. It suggests that children of this age are evaluative, expansive, have a very strong interest in adults, and that their relationship with adults is close but complex. It also shows that they are secretive and self-critical and that their feelings are easily hurt. The typical response also gives evidence that they are dramatic and explosive, emotionally impatient, demanding, egocentric, and much more outgoing than they were a year earlier.

REASONS OTHER THAN OVERPLACEMENT FOR SCHOOL DIFFICULTIES

If your girl or boy, at Eight or at any other age, is having serious difficulty in school, the diagnosis that you will be given depends a good deal on the historical period in which you live.

A few decades ago the school child who was having serious difficulty both with his work and his behavior was very often labeled *brain damaged.* Some mysterious damage was supposed to have occurred in his brain that made the child unable to function effectively. When most neurologists found it impossible to locate the specific damage, the term was gradually changed to *brain dysfunction,* which was perhaps more realistic but still did not get to the heart of the matter.

Some twenty years ago a new term came into our vocabulary. Boys or girls who do not do well in school now are customarily identified as being *learning disabled* (LD). Many child specialists find this a meaningful term, and certainly diagnosing and dealing with allegedly learning disabled boys and girls has become a profession in itself.

Our own difficulty with the term is that it is used all too loosely and all too widely. It is used as if a learning disability were a *thing* for which there is a simple remedy, such as putting the child into an LD class.

If your own child is having trouble in school and has been labeled LD, there are some things you might like to check—possible reasons he is having his difficulties. In our own clinical experience, the majority of children referred to us as learning disabled are those of basically normal endowment who are simply overplaced.

However, many children who are correctly placed gradewise may have other kinds of difficulties. Some are just not very bright. Though many schools tend to ignore this fact through mainstreaming, actually some children need to be in special classes rather than in the same classroom with boys and girls who are more normally endowed.

Often—and this is one of the more satisfactory reasons for difficulty because something constructive can often be done about it—there is something wrong with the child's biochemistry, something that can be helped by an improved diet or by protecting the child from substances to which he or she is allergic.

Very often, and here again something practical usually can be done, the child has a visual or a perceptual problem. We need to pay much more attention to the way the child uses his eyes. The fact that he may have been checked out as having adequate acuity (20/20 vision) gives no guarantee that he is using his eyes effectively.

Or the child may have a specific reading problem, or may indeed be one who is not academically well endowed and thus characteristically does poorly in all school subjects. In the 1970s Samuel Kirk, a recognized specialist in this field, noted that a review of 3,000 children enrolled in Child Service Demonstration Centers for Learning Disabilities in twenty-one states shows that most of the children so enrolled are general underachievers to a moderate degree in reading, spelling and/or math. He points out that one can raise the question of whether such underachievement constitutes anything that can be labeled a specific learning disability.

School difficulty could result from emotional disturbance, which can often be helped by psychotherapy.

An uneven endowment can be at the root of some school difficulties. Some children, even sometimes the highly gifted, are good in some areas of performance but woefully poor in others.

In some instances the teacher's teaching style does not fit with the child's learning style. Children are sometimes taught abstractly when their way of thinking is purely concrete.

At any rate, the term "learning disability" is quite certainly vastly overused these days. As the late Dr. Burton Blatt comments, "America seems to have fallen in love with minimal brain dysfunction or learning disability—a popular and even more up-to-date name for what used to be called brain injury." Many of us suspect that this relatively new term, though well intentioned, may be doing as much harm as good.

At any rate, if your boy or girl, at Eight or any age, is failing in school, it is essential that you as parent—either through the school's facilities or with the help of a child specialist in private practice—obtain a careful diagnosis and find out if you can specify what is wrong with your own child's functioning or with the school situation he is in. Without an adequate diagnosis it is difficult indeed to solve school problems.

Neither labeling a child as learning disabled nor mainstreaming one with serious difficulties on the assumption that being in the same room with children who *are* making it will in some mysterious way solve his difficulties is necessarily the answer.

At any rate, in summary, if your Eight-year-old *is* having real trouble in school, you and the school should check: the child's grade and class placement—is he ready for the grade he has been placed in?; does he need to be in a special class?; can inadequate or unsatisfactory behavior be the result of an allergic reaction to something in his diet or some other aspect of the environment?; does he have visual problems?; is a low intellect contributing to his difficulties?

While there nearly always is a sound reason for poor school performance, in most instances it is difficult to improve matters until one knows what that reason may be.

chapter eight
THE EIGHT-YEAR-OLD BIRTHDAY PARTY

Expansive! Speedy! Evaluative! This is the way we think of the typical Eight-year-old. All of these qualities have their advantages, but any of them can be a handicap when it comes to a party, unless taken into account in the party planning.

Expansive Eight looks for new fields to conquer—and enjoy! Thus if the party-givers so wish, a party for Eight-year-olds can extend beyond the confines of the host or hostess's home to include a trip to a nearby bowling alley or miniature golf range. (Or you can take them to a fast-food restaurant or some entertainment center and have the entire party outside the home—more expensive but a lot less work.) Even within the home, some new and unusual form of entertainment such as a magician's act might be offered successfully.

Speedy Eight will run through quite a lot of entertainment in a short time. No single activity should last overlong, and a good supply of different activities should be provided.

Evaluative Eight is a little less easily pleased than when he was younger, so that it is important to provide entertainment of a fairly high quality.

Eight's enthusiasm makes him an ideal party guest. Most come with goodwill and enjoy what is offered. A child may say, "I'd never miss a party!" However, especially if this is

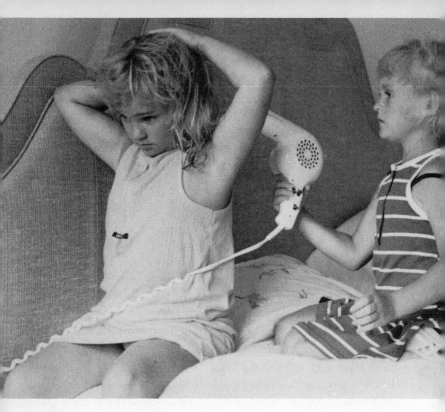

an all-boy party (and most boys of this age do not want girls), the presence of Father is very important to keep things from getting out of hand. If there is no father in the household, it is wise to seek the help of some other male friend or relative. If the party is all girls, Mother will need at least one adult helper.

Speed and energy are good qualities to have. Nevertheless, Eight's speed and energy (especially in boys) can provide a real menace at a party unless it is rather carefully planned, speedily conducted, and fully supervised. A houseful of roughhousing Eight-year-old boys has caused many a mother to vow "Never again!" after her son and his guests have turned the house into a shambles.

But the warmth, enjoyment, and full appreciation that Eight-year-olds feel and enthusiastically express at the end of a party that has been skillfully planned and conducted with their good traits, and limitations, in mind, make it evident that Eight *can be* an ideal age for a party.

KEYS TO SUCCESS

Planned entertainment, with alternating quiet and boisterous or active periods, is the secret of success at this age. Large blocks of activity will fill up the time happily and will avoid bedlam.

Number of guests: Six to eight guests is a good number, preferably all girls or all boys. Boys may be very definite about preferring "no girls," while girls may be willing to include boys. It may be well to overinvite, as children of this age have very busy schedules, and some guests may not make it.

Number of adults: Three adults are needed for this party—father (or other adult), mother, and helper with car.

SCHEDULE

This party could be given either in the morning (if on a weekend) or afternoon. The best hours may be from four to six, refreshments included.

4:00–5:00   Some planned away-from-home activity. Take the children to this right away. (Comic books may be read if there is any waiting.) Activities could be bowling at a bowling alley, miniature golf, hitting golf balls at a driving range. No prizes are needed for this part of the party.

5:00–5:30   Return home. Presents can be opened and then either a magician or just half an hour of games.

5:30–6:00   Refreshments. Choice of hamburgers or hot dogs on buns, raw carrots, potato chips, peanuts, milk (to be drunk through straws), ice cream or Popsicles, birthday cake. Table favors can be puzzle rings, so that children can play with them or swap them right at the table. Table conversation flows quite naturally but may at times need to be stimulated by adults. Decorations, especially balloons, add to the party atmosphere.

6:00   Party ends at the table. This is not too risky as the children will be fairly calm after eating. No planned activity is necessary for this period of parting. Some parents will call for their children, some guests can probably walk home alone. Any who have to wait could watch TV.

HINTS AND WARNINGS

As mentioned, a party for Eight-year-olds, especially boys, can turn into real bedlam unless planned and supervised carefully. Eight-year-olds are physically rather wild and boisterous. So plan every minute! And furthermore, plan what to do if guests come early. (They may arrive anywhere from an hour to a week early, so plan accordingly.) Also, if you plan for a magician and he arrives late, have a substitute activity planned. (Have all games planned carefully, with all equipment ready.)

Good games to be played if there is any time to be filled in are ball games, play with electric trains, or wrestling on mats. Still another is an old-fashioned game, such as Pin the Tail on the Donkey—or some modern version of this old favorite. Being blindfolded seems to add to the charm of this kind of game, and there will be much laughter when a child gets the tail in the wrong place.

As to the magician, if you choose to have one, it is better

to have no magician at all than a poor one. Eights are very skeptical and very critical. It works best for the magician to do quiet (but clever) things first to get the children's cooperation and to win over their initial skepticism. Children of this age are not primarily impressed with technical ability, but they do love to assist the magician. And as one famous man in this field has commented, "They are more impressed when the magician finds fifty-cent pieces behind their friends' ears than they would be if he produced a live elephant from a small box."

If you don't choose to have a magician or some other entertainer, fill in this time with planned competitive games, with prizes. No part of the program should last too long. Bowling should be no more than forty-five minutes, magician's act or games should not last more than half an hour.

With Eights, the main problem tends to be at the beginning of the party. They tend to relax as the party proceeds, and usually want to please the adults by the end of the party—particularly if they are having a good time. As they leave, Eights make very warm comments, such as "This was the most thrilling experience of my life."

Unlike the party for Seven-year-olds, which involves quite a series of different games, a party for Eights can consist of merely several large blocks of time, each filled with a single kind of more elaborate activity.

A PARTY FOR GIRLS

Actually you can have very much this same kind of party for girls. The chief difference is that girls are not as much of a menace at a party as are boys. They may become silly but are not as rough. Girls will enjoy bowling quite as well as boys if that is a chosen activity.

IF THE WHOLE PARTY IS GIVEN OUTSIDE THE HOME

Nowadays almost every community offers arrangements whereby a birthday party for children of almost any age can be held entirely outside the household if you prefer. Children may gather at the host's or hostess's house, leave presents, and then be transported to the spot where the party is to be held. There are usually many choices.

The cost of taking the children to a restaurant or amusement center varies, as does what will be provided. Some places provide entertainment, food, and all the paper goods —including invitations. Thus a fast-food restaurant may provide party favors (balloons, gifts) and a hostess who plays games with the children, as well as hamburgers or cheeseburgers, fries, soft drinks, and cake at about $2.50 per child for a party lasting one hour.

A local bowling alley may charge $10.00 to $20.00 per hour, per lane, and this will include shoes for participants. The alley may allow one hour for bowling and forty-five minutes at a picnic table behind the lanes, but you bring your own refreshments.

A Y may permit use of their swimming pool for an hour, then use of a kitchen area containing table and chairs, refrigerator, freezer, and stove. The charge per person is usually minimal.

chapter nine
STORIES FROM REAL LIFE

EIGHT-YEAR-OLD WANTS ALL OF MOTHER'S TIME AND ATTENTION

Dear Dr. Ames:

Ever since her father died six months ago, my Eight-year-old daughter, Melissa, has simply haunted me. She just doesn't let me out of her sight for a minute except, of course, when she is at school. But she won't go to the movies with anybody but me and won't even go out and play with her friends very much. She just hangs around the house and talks to me.

I'm afraid that she is getting some sort of an attachment or fixation on me, and it seems unhealthy. Might it be wise to take her to a psychiatrist to help her get over this attachment?

You have given an accurate description of what we have come to know as typical Eight-year-old behavior. The child of this age may literally haunt his mother. The child's need for a real relationship at this time is deep and demanding. And it is not only the mother's actions that are important to the Eight-year-old, but her very thoughts as well.

Eight's wish for closeness is so great that it often leads to his being "embroiled" with his mother. It seems to many mothers that their Eight-year-olds prefer even fighting with them to being left out of the relationship.

If this excessive demand for attention following the death of the child's father should go on through the years unabated, it might indeed be considered a danger signal. But we do not consider it dangerous when it occurs only around Eight years of age, as it appears in so many children in the normal course of growth.

Giving Melissa what she demands emotionally may be easier if you realize that this demand is a very important part of growing up to emotional maturity, even in children who have *not* experienced such a devastating loss. Melissa needs extra attention now; in time she will turn to other friends, but for now Mother is it.

When a child's parent dies, it is often wise to consider counseling, to help the child over this difficult period. If you suspect it would be useful for Melissa, by all means seek help.

DEFIANT EIGHT-YEAR-OLD SON'S ATTITUDE WORRIES MOTHER

Dear Dr. Ames:

I have read and reread all you have written on Eight-year-old behavior. Ours is a textbook case! My particular problem is the defiance—and what seems like sheer hatred toward me—every time it is necessary for me to correct our son, or to forbid something that will either hurt him or someone else or someone's property, all of which seems to happen all day long. I often end up with giving in to him when he shrieks at me about not loving him or not caring about what makes him happy. Then I hate myself for not sticking to my own convictions.

He is a sensitive child and feels many things very deeply. He loves his father, thank goodness, and respects

his authority. But he seems to feel so bitter toward me. Yet he won't let me out of his sight. He spends many Saturdays with his father in the office. This he adores and he is good from morning till night, pleasing his father at every turn.

He is a bright, intelligent child, gentle in so many ways and good at heart. But any refusal that I must give him is always met with a torrent of condemnation of his mother as the "meanest person around, who doesn't care ever about what I like . . ." etc., etc.

Should I just look forward to the better age of Nine? Or is there something I can do now to make him feel that the world, and especially his mother, isn't against him?

There are many good things about your son's situation. One of the best, of course, is his excellent relationship with his father. This will do more than anything else to get him through this difficult Eight-year-old period.

As you know from your reading, Eight-year-olds are quite normally all mixed up with their mothers. The mother-child relationship at this age is one of the strongest, deepest, most demanding, and yet most tangled to date. The apparent strength of their occasional seeming hatred for their mother often tends to mark the strength of their dependence on her. Even by Nine, most children are a little more ready to let their mothers be and not take everything out on them.

About the best a mother can do is to lovingly adopt a rather hard-boiled attitude toward a boy of this age. Whenever his own behavior will allow it, be as completely understanding as you can. But when he starts "taking things out" on you, let him see, if you can possibly steel yourself to it, that this is not crushing you. It is no fun to take things out on somebody who is not harmed.

Of course, this dual course is hard to steer. At the same time that you have to protect yourself against him, he needs to know that you really love him, understand him, sympathize with him. It is a tangle that usually only age solves. But it doesn't help the tangle if you get all mixed up too.

Have him with his father or otherwise away from home as much as you can manage for the next few months. Try to be with him in situations where you can devote pretty nearly 100 percent of your time and attention to him, and try to be doing positive things together.

EIGHT-YEAR-OLD SON'S BELLIGERENCE, DECEIT, AND
POOR SCHOOLWORK CONCERN PARENTS

Dear Dr. Ames:

My husband and I are older parents (in our forties) and
we have several what seem to us very troublesome problems with our Eight-year-old son, Matthew. His problem
behaviors include the following: He does badly in school
—not because of lack of ability but because he doesn't
concentrate. Also, he is belligerent, talks back, lies, and is
deceitful. He doesn't accept punishment and is very belligerent about it. When we criticize him he raises his
voice and curls his lips in an awful sneer. When he is
doing something bad, often he won't stop until we use
force, and even then he will do the bad thing "just one
more time." His table manners are bad, and we find it
necessary to pick on him a good deal at mealtime.

Though it would be a lot more dramatic for us to say we
think that Matthew needs the help of a child specialist, we
have to admit that his behavior doesn't sound much worse
to us than that of a good many other perfectly normal boys
of his age.

Sometimes when there is only one child, and the parents
are in their forties, more pressure is put on the child than
you realize. We don't begin to mean that you are the cause
of your son's unruly behavior. We just suggest that if he
were one of half a dozen, or if you were a lot younger, some
of his rebellious behavior would not occur.

Many children behave as Matthew does about this time,
calm down around ten, and then start in the series of erup-
tions that in many constitute adolescence. We think the
first thing to do might be to let up on your son a little at
mealtimes. We don't mean spoil or pamper him or let him
do anything he wants to. But just figure out which of the

orders, directions, commands you could reasonably skip. Then, having reduced orders to a minimum, be sure that you enforce those you do give.

As to his lying—try to reduce the situations in which he lies. Don't ask him if he hung up his clothes. Don't ask him if he washed his hands. Many boys answer many routine questions like this with untruths. If he can't be trusted to carry notes, information, money, from home to teacher, just explain to him that you will have to take care of these things yourself and that when he is a little older and can be trusted, he will again be given the responsibility.

As for his schoolwork, without seeing him we cannot, of course, tell you why he does so badly. We can say that in most of the poor-schoolwork cases we see clinically, there is usually a very good reason why the child does as badly as he does. Are you sure that he is correctly placed in school? At Eight and a half he may be ready only for second-grade performance. Like many boys, he may be able to do the actual schoolwork but may not be able to meet the total requirements of the grade.

WORRIED CHILD HATES TO LEAVE MOTHER

Dear Dr. Ames:

My son Kenneth, almost eight, has suddenly turned from an outgoing child into a real worrywart and a real clinger. He complains and worries all the time and also clings to me terribly. He follows me around and is so terribly affectionate. He hates to part from me to go to school, and also doesn't want to leave me to go to bed. He is afraid that something will "get" him in the night.

Is there anything I can do to eliminate his fears of bedtime, to make our parting more pleasant in the morning, and to detach him somewhat from me? His sisters think he's quite impossible and make fun of him and his fears.

Your problem is extremely interesting because Kenneth is showing outstanding characteristics of both Seven and Eight years of age. This is pretty tough on him and very hard on you. Usually children get over the worrisome, anxious Seven-year-old stage before they fall into the clinging, demanding, won't-let-Mother-out-of-their-sight habits of Eight.

You of course must be firm and let your son know that he does have to go to school. He's probably right that the days are too long. Could you arrange, as is often done with younger children, that he have one afternoon a week off— perhaps Wednesdays?

Then, to help answer his strong need for your company, could you go back to the procedure that many parents follow with younger children of having one afternoon a week (perhaps that same Wednesday) be his time with you? He could be allowed to plan in advance and to choose what treats or excursions you could enjoy together.

Sometimes the daily morning parting can be helped if you give him a "secret" note, which he can carry in his pocket and open at recess. Or provide any other device that will give him the feeling that you are thinking especially of him.

This may seem that you're giving in to his whim, but right now Kenneth does feel lonely, fatigued, unloved, and very dependent on you. When and if you do give in to demands like his (for less school, more of your attention), you gradually explain to him that after a little while he won't need so much help and protection. That is, you make it evident that any palliative measure is only temporary.

As to his sisters' making fun of him, it's tough on him, true. But in a way, that is one of the advantages of family life. Even when parents may and do to some extent give in to a child's weaknesses, there are his siblings making it evident that the world does make rather firm demands.

They provide a refreshing and useful breath of reality—even though one that is seldom appreciated by the victim.

EIGHT-YEAR-OLD BOY REALLY NEEDS SOLACE OF HIS FUR DOG

Dear Dr. Ames:

I am writing to you about our Eight-year-old. He was a very jumpy baby. Getting him to sleep was always a big problem, and once he was asleep we really tiptoed around. Friends and relatives told us we should get him used to noise. But they didn't have to listen to him howl when a noise would waken him.

He was also a child you could not prepare for new experiences. It seemed better to tell him at the last minute with no time to back out. Well-meaning friends would talk to him about going to school, how nice, how much fun. Immediately he would get a suspicious look in his eye, and if they persisted he would break out in tears and say he didn't want to go. He is now in third grade and quite a problem for his teacher. Every fall he starts the year by bursting into tears at the least little thing. The teacher says he is capable if he would only buckle down and concentrate.

Ever since he was a baby he has taken a fur dog to bed with him and rubs his face in it. This really did help him to go to sleep. Now it seems as if he can't watch TV without it. Nothing makes my husband madder than to see that great big hulk of a boy drooping around with a fur dog in his face. Lately we have made quite an issue of it. But since we have put the pressure on, he has become even more talkative and fidgety at school. Should we go ahead and let him have his fur dog? Will he ever give it up on is own?

Your son has a very interesting and certainly a very definite personality of his own. We think you understand him very well. You were wise to protect him from noise when he was little, and from knowing about situations in advance. In fact, your letter brings out most clearly how important it is for parents—who know their own children better than any outsider does—to stick to their guns and not take too much advice from other people. Friends told you that you should get him used to noise. You knew he wasn't ready. They talked to him in advance about impending activities. You knew that he needed to be protected from too much planning in advance. This kind of child needs to be protected for a longer time than others.

Now, as to his dependence on his fur dog, we sympathize with your husband's reaction to this behavior. However, we suspect that for the time being your son needs this solace until other tensions are relaxed. Then help him to plan to give it up and possibly substitute something such as clay that he can play with in his hands as he watches television. Or he might wish to purchase a little rabbit good-luck charm that he could keep in his pocket, instead of having his dog. This may seem a little peculiar, but some children do really depend on these soft, fuzzy objects.

MOTHER HAS CONSTANT BATTLE BECAUSE DAUGHTER IS SO MESSY

Dear Dr. Ames:

I am involved in a never-ending battle with my Eight-year-old daughter, Megan. She not only refuses to keep her room clean but absolutely refuses to pick up anything. Toys are strewn around, books never put back in the shelves, her clothes are all over the place. We fight about this constantly.

With my two older children this problem never really came up. My oldest is a boy, so it is natural that I should pick up after him. And my Twelve-year-old girl, though not really neat, is not too bad. Just the little one, and it's gotten to the point that I don't know what to do about her.

Your letter brings out several important points. First, that mothers often don't have as many daily battles with their sons as with their daughters because often they don't expect as much of their sons. Your boy isn't neat around the house but it doesn't make any problem because you don't really expect him to be.

It also suggests that a child's neatness or lack of it (like so many other behaviors) is not entirely a result of upbringing. The older of your girls is reasonably neat by nature, so there's no big problem there.

But your younger girl is messy, and with her (unlike the case with your boy) you have decided that it's time now to crack down. And it's getting you nowhere.

We too favor neatness. But sometimes it's best to know when you're beaten, at least temporarily. If it takes five times as much energy to get a child to hang up her coat as it would to hang it up yourself, and if in spite of your efforts she isn't improving anyway, sometimes it seems wisest to give up on the effort. Give up now and try again later.

Some mothers do manage to achieve at least a reasonable degree of neatness by instituting a system of fines—so much for each garment found out of place. Or at least so much for anything left in the living room that doesn't belong there. However, any such system usually works well only at first. Then Mother forgets to insist on the fines and soon things are as messy as ever.

If you think you can carry it through, you might insist on one or two small bits of neatness from Megan. But for the most part, you might tell her that you have come to realize that she isn't old enough to be truly neat, just yet. And bargain with her: If she will hang up her coat, for instance, and keep her toys out of the living room except when she is playing with them, you'll let up on her room and other issues. For the time being.

You still have one old-fashioned method to try. Tidy up her room with her. A little camaraderie goes a long way, and you may find she enjoys this time with you. This may work much better than forcing her to do it alone.

FATHER CRITICIZES GIRL FOR USING HER LEFT HAND

Dear Dr. Ames:

I have never seen or heard my problem discussed, and hope you can help me. My Eight-year-old daughter is left-handed. That in itself is no problem to me as I feel it is perfectly normal for some children to be left-handed. But my husband constantly refers to it, in front of her, as if it were an affliction. If she picks up a ball and throws it with her right hand, then he wants to know why she can't write with her right hand.

Amanda is an exceptionally bright child, always in the top third in her class. But she is also very sensitive and extremely anxious to be accepted as one of her crowd. That is why I am concerned over the effects of her father's remarks upon her. One afternoon, after completing her written homework in fifteen minutes, she struggled for another hour doing it with her right hand.

The situation is becoming quite nerve-wracking for me. I have been biting my tongue to keep mealtime pleasant for the last few years, every time my husband mentions that Amanda is holding the knife in the wrong hand when she cuts her meat. Or perhaps I'll put something on the fork for my younger child and without thinking I'll place it at the left side of her plate. My husband then tells me I'm trying to make the little one left-handed too.

You are quite right, of course, that your daughter's being left-handed is no problem in itself. The problem is that her father mentions it and makes an issue of it. Of course it is hard for grownups to change, but if your husband could only realize how much harm he is doing, perhaps he would bite *his* tongue and not speak whenever he feels impelled to mention her left-handedness.

Amanda should be assured that it is perfectly normal and all right to use her left hand. In the case of very young children with a tendency to be ambidextrous, it does no harm for the parents to help them use the right hand instead of the left, especially for eating. This is one area where there is most comment and most inconvenience, and where the shift to using the right hand may in some cases not be too difficult.

By Amanda's age, handedness is usually well established. In her case her preference seems to have been evident quite early. She was born that way. You may even recall that in the early weeks of life, as she lay on her back she tended to turn her head toward her left side and to stretch out her left arm. If you and her father look over some of her baby pictures, you might be able to note this, and he might just possibly be able to change his attitude, knowing that she was that way from the beginning. A conference with the teacher might help your husband to accept his daughter's left-handedness.

NOT ALL BED-WETTERS ARE EMOTIONALLY DISTURBED

Dear Dr. Ames:

Bless you for your recent suggestion that not all cases of bed-wetting are caused by emotional disturbance. We get so tired of being told that our Eight-year-old son wets his bed because he is emotionally disturbed.

Erik is eight and in third grade, overplaced of course but still getting along. He usually wets two hours after bedtime and again around three A.M. He is a very sound sleeper. For several years we have tried getting him up in the evening, but he can't find his own way to the bathroom or back to bed. He has numerous bet-wetting cousins.

We are all fed up with the problem and eager to tackle it. But we can tolerate it a little longer if you think we should wait. We have checked with a urologist who assures us that there appears to be nothing physically wrong with our son.

You obviously have a difficult problem on your hands if your son is Eight and still wetting two hours after bedtime and again around three A.M. Also if he is such a sound sleeper and if there is a family history of bed-wetting.

With younger children we usually advise that it is worthwhile taking the child to the bathroom two or three hours after bedtime if this insures dryness for the rest of the night. But it is not worthwhile if it doesn't.

As Erik is still expressing a preschool pattern of both early and late night wetting, his organism seems to be a long way from being ready to stay dry by itself. He has now passed the deadline of time when we rather expect children to have nighttime bladder control. Therefore, it could be time to try one of the good conditioning-devices now available, such as an alarm that is set off by wetness when the child urinates. We see the use of a conditioning device as not so much a way of curing something wrong as a way of giving the child's organism a little nudge toward a maturity of functioning that it is approaching but hasn't made by itself.

We would check with the school as to the possibility of putting him back into second grade to see if the removal of everyday stresses and strains might help him attain dryness on his own. The two things may not seem to be related. However, night wetting is not only a result of immaturity

—it can sometimes be a response to a life that is too demanding.

And here are two typical letters from relieved mothers of (now) dry boys.

When I told my Eight-year-old, Timmy, about the device you recommended, he eagerly showed me an advertisement in one of the mail-order catalogs for just such a device. Since they seemed about the same, we sent for the one he had discovered himself. He really couldn't wait to begin.

The first week was hectic and disappointing. Timmy was setting the alarm off three times a night with his wetting and I was busy stripping the bed and making it up afresh. But after just a few nights of all this chaos, we began to have an occasional dry night. At the end of a month we had twelve dry nights in a row—this after literally never having had a dry night in his whole life.

For a while we disconnected the machine and then tried a final week before we removed it completely. He was wet on the fourth day, dry for six days, and then wet once more. He was really angry. But after we pointed out his tremendous improvement and what a miracle the whole thing was, he calmed down and gamely started out on our seven-day goal again. This time he succeeded and the gadget is now in the attic, stripped of its batteries for which he has found other uses. We are a delighted household.

A second mother reports briefly on the same story of initial chaos and subsequent rather rapid success, as follows.

We tried the conditioning device you mentioned for our Eight-year-old, Jeff. The buzzer agitated him quite a bit at first. He would try to hide under the sheet when it went off. Then he would put his hands over his ears and draw his legs up, trying to get away from the noise.

But I would help him to put his hand on the switch and turn if off. By the second week, he would turn it off himself. By the end of the second week he was dry, but we continued for another week just to make sure.

All this time his daddy and sisters and brothers and I all praised him whenever he had a dry night and earned a gold star. I shall be forever grateful to you for that article on bed-wetting. It has changed our whole household.

EIGHT-YEAR-OLD BOY AFRAID AT BEDTIME

Dear Dr. Ames:

I have an Eight-year-old son, David. David is afraid of staying in his own room at night, even with a night-light on. Things like a robot, a small little man with large black eyes, are running around after him. They are not always dreams, because frequently he does not even fall asleep before he is bounding into the living room in fear. When they happen during the night he gets into bed with me and goes right off to sleep until morning. At first they were only occasional, but now this happens almost every night.

David is a bright little boy—presents no problems in school, is fine at all times until bedtime. He enjoys his playmates, games, and all normal boy play. He is the youngest of five. I have not had this trouble with any of the others. I might add that this has been going on for only about six months. Staying with him, talking and comforting him, do no good.

Also, I note from one of your books that Eight-year-olds are usually good eaters. David has never been a good one—a well-planned meal means nothing to him, so that he has spoiled the meals for the rest of us until now, when I try to give him what appeals to him within reason.

Your son's behavior is more like that of a Seven-year-old than an Eight. Many Sevens do go through a brief period of being extremely fearful at bedtime. They think there are ghosts or robbers in the closet. The shadows on the wall scare them. Or they think that animals are going to hurt them.

This is not, in most cases, anything to be much worried about in itself. (That is, if there are no further symptoms and if it does not continue too long.) With very young children we sometimes pretend to exorcise the animals or the ghost. If your son has a good sense of humor you might try that for him. With others, a flashlight under the pillow may help. First you show them that there is nothing in the closet or under the bed. Then you leave them with a low light on and with their flashlight handy.

You don't try to convince them that there is nothing there—it isn't a matter of argument. Just take it sympathetically but lightly. Give reasonable proof that the child is safe, and then leave the rest up to him! But at the same time appreciate that there will still be times when he will need to come out into the living room or into your bedroom.

These disturbances are usually not dreams. They occur while the child is still awake, or half asleep. Of course, if this fear continues, and increases to tremendous proportions, you might need to get some therapeutic help for your boy. But this is seldom necessary. Most outgrow this kind of fear.

As to his eating, we have found that many poor eaters do improve a great deal around Eight years of age. In his case, we would hope for this improvement around Nine. Several other parents have complained to us that their children's appetite did not improve at Eight. Well, of course we give no guarantee. Alas, some children never improve very much but remain small and fussy eaters.

BOY HAS TROUBLE GETTING TO SLEEP

Dear Dr. Ames:

My Eight-year-old son, Tony, is a highly strung, alert, and active child, and we have a serious sleep problem. Even after a very quiet evening, he has difficulty in going to sleep, often thrashes about in his bed and will even weep, until eleven or eleven thirty. Is there any way I can combat this getting-to-sleep difficulty? Can you at least offer me consolation? I had this difficulty of getting to sleep all my life.

Tony is a busy-minded boy. Even while he watches TV he must be reading a comic book, building with blocks, or playing with cards. Should I simply let him play in his room till he gets sleepy, rather than having this long lights-out time?

Your son does have a real problem. (You also mention that he is enuretic.) This suggests that here is a rather immature organism who if he isn't having difficulty in one direction will be likely to have it in another.

It sounds as though Tony might be a boy of a somewhat ectomorphic (or angular and slender) physique. This is the kind of body that usually has the most trouble in getting to sleep. In any event, we do think it would help you, and Tony, if you both could understand his basic personality better. And to know that it is normal for some people to have trouble getting to sleep.

It's true, from what you say, that Tony is getting less than the average amount of sleep for a boy his age. But keep in mind that the sleep requirements of different people vary tremendously. Some need much less than others.

We would recommend a slightly later bedtime, and then

be certain to allow for a little quieting-down time, during which he reads and/or listens to his radio. Try to help Tony accept the fact that it may take at least an hour of this quieting-down time before he can expect to get to sleep. If he didn't worry about *not* sleeping, the whole situation would not seem so hard to him.

We suspect that your son's sleeping problem may be only part of the whole story of an immature, tense little boy. We suspect you can't solve just one part of his problem separately.

I'm sorry that we can't tell you, specifically, how to get your son to sleep. But his wakefulness sounds like just part of a rather complex problem. And, as you say, he comes by his sleep problem honestly, as you yourself have suffered from this and never solved it.

EIGHT-YEAR-OLD STILL SUFFERS FROM EFFECTS OF EARLY ABUSE

Dear Dr. Ames:

My Eight-year-old daughter, Elsa, lately has had terribly frightening dreams that upset her greatly. She dreams that a man is chasing her. "I don't want him to hurt you, Mummy, like he hurt me," she says when she awakes and I hold her close and try to comfort her.

I asked her to tell me all about the dream, but she always hesitates and won't say any more than that he caught her.

How far does a parent go in trying to persuade a child to tell such a dream in detail? What approach helps most with a frightened child? It is only recently that she has had these frightening dreams. In the past her dreams have been no worse than those of other children, so far as I know.

This precious blessing was molested by a man when she was only Two and a half years old. So I naturally worry as to how much she remembers of that horrible experience and if it will repeat itself in her dreams.

I have asked her about schoolmates and friends, and she seems to like them all and also likes school. I do control what she sees on TV, as with all my children. Please give me some answer as to what to say to a child awakened by a bad dream. Of course I offer her love; this I do naturally.

Some children do have bad dreams as a result of things they see on television. Girls seem, TV or not, often to dream of men under their beds or men looking in the window. However, in view of the fact that your daughter did have this unfortunate experience and that she is still dreaming of men hurting her, we would be inclined to seek the benefit of a little psychotherapy. We know less than we should about the emotional effects of child abuse, but nowadays we take this kind of experience very seriously. It is reasonable to hope that a good therapist could help your daughter work out any fears and anxieties that she may be experiencing as a result of this early incident.

GRANDMOTHER TRIES TO IMPROVE HER GRANDCHILDREN

Dear Dr. Ames:

I have two grandchildren whom I love dearly, but they both have serious faults. The little girl, Christine, is almost Four but she still sucks her thumb. The boy, James, is Eight and his manners are very lax. He very seldom says "please" or "thank you." Since their parents do almost nothing about these faults, I have taken it on myself to try to correct them.

It is hard for me to believe that my daughter and her husband are so casual about these behaviors. Not only casual, but they even tell me, in a polite way, to skip it, that they will do whatever needs to be done. Don't you agree that it is my privilege, as well as my responsibility, to step in, since the parents are failing to do so?

You talk about "serious faults." If you would visit any child behavior clinic in your community you could see really serious faults. True, you may not like to see Christine sucking her thumb. And it may very well bother you that James isn't very mannerly. But these will undoubtedly pass with time.

If your daughter and her husband should tell you that they were working on these problems and would appreciate your help, fine and good. But since, as you say, they are very casual about these matters, I personally, as a grandmother myself, would butt out.

EIGHT-YEAR-OLD A FIRE-SETTER

Dear Dr. Ames:

We are the parents of seven children and have the usual number of problems and pleasures. Our current greatest problem is our Eight-year-old son, Benjy, who has been setting fires. His setting some rags on fire in our upstairs bathroom last night was the culmination of at least three years of worry and concern for him.

The immediate solution will, of course, be unflagging vigilance. But in spite of the seriousness of this act, we do not look on this as just a misbehavior. Rather we think of it as just one more symptom of an unhappy boy. Perhaps it is Nature's way of warning us that we must do something about Benjy.

Actually, though my husband and I get on well with each other, we are not terribly adequate people. Before we can help our son, so much like his father, perhaps we need help ourselves. We wondered if we should start by seeking a marriage counselor.

You are wise parents to realize that punishing a fire-setter is not the solution. It does no harm to punish him, but, if you do so, you would have to realize that it's only a first step and not particularly constructive.

A very young child may play with matches if they're available simply because they are there. But when an Eight-year-old sets a fire, even a small one, you're right— he is in trouble. It may indeed be his way of calling for help.

You ask about seeing a marriage counselor. We would prefer a family counselor who would work with the two of you, with Benjy, and possibly with other family members. The alternative would be to start with Benjy, alone. How about looking to the school for help? Do they have either a school psychologist or a guidance counselor? If so, at least you could try a conference with them and see what they have to say about your son.

If you can't get help directly at school, they should be able to refer you to a good local psychologist or child guidance clinic. Even when you find this service, things aren't necessarily going to clear up overnight. But usually they do improve.

And just the fact that you're taking this much interest in Benjy may please him and help him.

GIVE MONEY–DEMANDING EIGHT–YEAR–OLD OPPORTUNITY TO EARN FOR HIMSELF

Dear Dr. Ames:

Our Eight-year-old son seems to think of absolutely nothing but money, money, money, and buy me, buy me, buy me, until both his father and I are nearly at our wits' end.

Every time be receives his weekly allowance, all he can think of is to dash off madly to the store and spend the entire amount, and then he'll tease continuously for more money to buy himself trivial little toys until his next allowance day, when the same old routine begins again.

My husband and I have gotten to the point where we hate taking him shopping with us, for he's never satisfied with anything for ten minutes after he has it. He just sees something else to start begging for. And when he doesn't get it, he will start crying and putting up a fuss until clerks, and patrons too, will look at us and make us feel so embarrassed.

We have pointed out to him that few children get even as much as he does. We have given him certain tasks to be performed around the house for which he is not paid, but have listed other tasks that he may do for extra money if he chooses to. We have even told him he must go to the car and wait for us if he puts up a scene in a store. Nothing works.

You can at least have the satisfaction of knowing that your son, in his overenthusiasm for money, is behaving in a manner characteristic of his age. Parents are often disturbed by the "money mad" interest of the typical Eight-year-old boy, but they should not underestimate the motivation value of this same interest. Here is an excellent opportunity to use a stimulus, which at the same time also serves to give a child some idea of money values.

That is, his attitude, even though unattractive, is quite normal for his age. He will undoubtedly be more reasonable, even if not less enthusiastic, about money in another year or two.

In the meantime, you have to be firm and not let him get away with too much. But at the same time, if possible, give him more opportunity to earn money. Even the minimal household tasks could be rewarded financially. Stick to whatever boundaries you set, but give him the opportunity to earn, and even give him the necessary push to set about doing the work offered.

He is behaving in a rather immature way in the stores, admittedly. When he acts this way, know that he is not ready to be taken with you. You say you have tried leaving him home but it hasn't "worked." Well, it isn't going to work the first time, or perhaps even the fifth, but eventually it is almost certain to. Tell him that he may go as soon as he is ready to behave himself.

You say you would like him to be more appreciative of what he has. We're afraid that you may have quite a long way to go before he is as appreciative as you would like him to be. Many boys and girls are fully Sixteen before they begin to show this kind of appreciation. In the long run, the trend is toward improvement. You just have to make your rules, stick to your standards, and not expect too much or be too easily discouraged.

NEW BABY IN THE HOME PROBABLY RESPONSIBLE FOR EIGHT-YEAR-OLD'S INTEREST IN SEX

Dear Dr. Ames:

My problem concerns my Eight-year-old son, and I would appreciate any help you can give me. We have had a fine relationship up to now, and I'm trying to keep in mind that Eight-year-olds are often on the difficult side.

I found him crying one night after he had gone to bed, and he told me he was thinking of all the bad words he had used when he was a small boy. He was sorry he had said them. I explained that at the time he was too young to know what he was saying; that he was much older now and could just forget about it. I told him if he was disturbed about anything to come to me and I'd try to help him out.

Since then he's nearly driven me crazy. He talks of sex all the time. He likes to look at little girls' pants, and it has got so I'm getting self-conscious when he comes into the room. He tells me he can see my slip. He's telling me all his thoughts, and the thing I don't understand is, he asks the same questions over and over.

This is my first brush with sex questions and I'm baffled. I have a small baby, a few months old. Do you think this caused the curiosity? How do I cope with this? Can you suggest anything? My husband laughs it off, but I'm the one our son talks to.

He's exceptionally religious for his age, and there seems to be a conflict between the two interests. He talks of love of God continually, and in the next breath talks of sex. Is it just his awakening to sex? How can I explain things to him? Can you suggest some book I can read or let him read? My husband seems to feel that all this is just his way of attracting attention because of the baby, but I don't think so. There seems to be a conflict in his mind between good and bad.

I'd be most grateful for your answer. It bothers me to see him so disturbed.

Your son sounds like a nice little boy, already aware of the meaning of what he calls "bad" words. He really seems to want to be good. He does show a slightly excessive interest in sex, though it is not too unusual for boys of this age to be interested in peeping, smutty jokes, girls' underwear, and so on. Having a new baby in the family has undoubtedly intensified his interest in and emotional response to the whole matter of sex.

A chatting time at bedtime may be the best opportunity for giving him the information he seeks. With the lights out you may feel more comfortable in talking about these things with him. Do answer his questions fully. You can usually tell if you are telling too much because the child who is being overinformed tends to lose interest in the conversation.

Once he has all the main facts about babies—how they get in and how they get out—straightened out in his mind, this talking will probably fall off. But it is a good sign that he will talk. He seems to feel a real conflict about good and bad, and talking should help him to resolve this. We don't, of course, know what facts he has absorbed about religion, but they do seem to be complicating things for him.

As for a book to read, libraries and bookstores are full of reliable books about sex and babies. Our favorite is Peter Mayle's *Where Did I Come From?* It is clear, factual, and very, very amusing. If it is a little too frank for you, your local librarian should certainly be able to find something that will be comfortable for you to share.

IS THE TERM "FUNNY UNCLE" FAIR?

Dear Dr. Ames:

As an affectionate bachelor uncle who enjoys showing physical warmth to my young nieces and nephews, I take great exception to the term that you columnists use so freely—"Funny Uncle." I think you do us a great disservice. Not every uncle who likes to hug or kiss these young people has evil designs in mind. And, of course, as the children grow older and are less welcoming of a physical show of affection, I use common sense and back off.

I myself am not a user of this term but I know all too well what is meant. And although it may not apply to you, it's important for people to recognize that, according to some figures, in this country a child is sexually abused at the rate of one every two minutes, by relatives or strangers.

This isn't necessarily just happening to somebody else's children—it could be your own. Thus we welcome any help parents can get to protect their boys and girls from this abuse.

Sometimes we think that this kind of abuse comes just from outside the family. However, as Robin Lennett points out in an extremely useful book, *It's OK to Say No,* the typical child molester is not a stranger as is commonly believed. Most child molesters know their victims. They are relatives, family friends, neighbors, or someone else the child encounters routinely.

Lennett gives lots of practical advice to parents. Perhaps the book's important message is that you should teach your child that he has the right to say no to anyone who puts him in a situation that feels uncomfortable. And that "no" should be sufficient. The child does not need to explain.

One charming (and extremely useful) part of this book is a series of stories parents can read to, and then discuss with, their children. For instance, while Billy was walking home from school a lady in a car asks him if he wants a ride. He knows that he should never get into a car without his mom or dad's permission, so he says no and runs home. (Then you ask your child what he would have done in this situation.)

Or a grocery store man offers Mary Ann a present "because you are so nice." The girl says "No, thank you" and runs home. (Again, after reading this story, you ask your own child what she would have done in this case.)

These lessons are, we think, acceptable, unfrightening, and effective because they are presented in dialogue form. We strongly recommend this book. We also recommend another, on the same subject, but with quite a different presentation. *Chilly Stomach* by Jeanette Caines tells a story that could happen to any family, even your own. A little girl doesn't like it when her Uncle Jim tickles her and hugs her and kisses her. When he does these things she gets a chilly stomach. Her family doesn't seem to notice, and she doesn't dare to tell how she feels for fear they will be angry at her, or might think she is making a fuss about nothing. But she does tell her friend Jill, who is going to tell her mother about it. The girl hopes that Jill's mother will tell her own parents.

This book might open quite a few eyes. I hope it will.

As to child abuse in general, not just sexual abuse, here's one more bit of information I'd like to share. Pediatrics professor Kim Oates from the University of Sydney lists several widely held "myths" about child abuse:

Medical practitioners are automatically child-abuse experts.

Professional services alone can solve the problem.

Child abuse is equally distributed in all social classes.

All families can be helped.

Removing the child from the family is always the answer.

The law is on the side of the child.

Teaching high-school students principles of good parenting will solve the problem.

HOW ABOUT SEX EDUCATION IN SCHOOLS?

Dear Dr. Ames:

I would like to know your views on sex education in the public schools. In our town this has always been a very hot issue, but now the whole matter is heating up even more. There are tremendous extremes of opinion. Some say, "No sex education at all." Others insist we must have it. Some say "Just the facts, please." Others feel that we must include values. Some stand for just discussions of "normal," everyday sex. Others favor the inclusion of any and all aberrations, including a full discussion of AIDS. Help!

We at Gesell have always favored sex education in the schools. Even kindergarten children ask questions that need to be answered. For the most part, we have found that those parents who are most against sex education in school are the ones who, at home, do the poorest job of providing needed information. Calm, confident parents who themselves actually do well at providing information at home tend to be quite welcoming of any supplementary help the school may provide.

We tend to prefer the kind of sex education that not only provides necessary information but that supports the values about sexual behavior which most homes and most religious groups favor—so-called absolute values, which support responsibility in sexual relations. A government-sponsored group called SIECUS for a time favored the teaching of "relative" values—supporting the notion that whatever you enjoy is good for you and that reasonable chastity and abstinence are no better than promiscuity. Fortunately, we hear less from SIECUS than we used to.

A new controversy, however, has to do not so much with whether facts about sex should or should not be taught as to whether facts about unconventional sex should be included. Especially with the current threat of AIDS, some believe that even third-graders should be taught about extreme versions of sexual activity, such as anal sex.

We feel that AIDS should be covered, but ideally *not* the less conventional kinds of sexual activity. In our experience, most Eight-year-olds are mature enough to understand explanations as to where babies come from. Not all, so far as we have observed, are fully ready to understand the father's part, at least in any detail. It seems unwise to us, with children this young, to go beyond a description of customary intercourse.

No matter what we as adults may think about unconventional sex activities, the maturity or immaturity of the child being taught should always be a prime consideration. The average Eight-year-old tends to be sexually quite unsophisticated.

SHOULD YOU PAY CHILDREN FOR DOING CHORES?

Dear Dr. Ames:

I realize that you have probably answered this question many times through the years. But I suppose it is always new for new parents. We have three children ages Six, Eight, and Nine. We have always paid them for household chores. Not for every single little thing they do, but for their "regular" tasks, such as taking out trash, setting the table, helping with dishes, and so on. This is the way I was brought up and it seems sensible to us.

Now all of a sudden my mother-in-law says we are doing things all wrong. That the children should get a set allowance, which is their part or share of the family money. And that they should do household chores for free, as *their* part of family living.

Who is right?

In our opinion there is no definite right or wrong in this matter. Some families are most comfortable to give their children a set allowance. Many share your mother-in-law's rather fanciful notion that children should "want" to help out and do their share of family tasks. Giving an allowance may in many cases be the easiest way—certainly it involves less bookkeeping. But many families follow your own plan with good success. And some combine the two methods—give a set allowance that can then be bolstered up by doing special tasks for pay. So our advice is, do what comes naturally to you and your husband and your children and don't worry about your mother-in-law. It is not her problem.

BOY DESTROYS REPORT CARD AND THEN
LIES ABOUT IT

Dear Dr. Ames:

My wife and I are extremely concerned about our Eight-year-old son, Brian. Brian is in third grade and is not doing well in school. He moves around too much, they say, and can't seem to copy things correctly, either from the board or from papers on his desk.

We're sorry about this but do realize that not all children star academically. What worries us is that recently he has been tearing up his report cards and then lying about it. Says the teacher didn't give them to him. Up till now Brian has always told the truth, and we are very upset about his lying.

Some schools mail the report cards home and that would take care of that, wouldn't it? Actually we would be much more concerned about why your son is having such a hard time in school than about his not bringing his report card home and then lying about it.

Nobody really knows how scared Brian may be about bringing home a poor report. You sound like a reasonable man, but your son may be terrified of you when he gets bad grades. That is what would concern us. Brian may be, like so many, merely overplaced. Or, because he can't copy correctly, he may have a specific visual problem. Or if he moves around "too much," he may be what people call (though not always correctly) hyperactive.

Talk to the school and if they can't come up with an answer, take your son to a good child specialist or clinic and get a careful diagnosis. It will be hard for you to solve Brian's problem till you know what it really is.

IS THIS BOY REALLY HYPERACTIVE?

Dear Dr. Ames:

The school tells me that our second son, Joe, now in third grade, is definitely hyperactive and that we should do something about it. On the other hand our pediatrician, who has known Joe since birth and also knows his brothers, says that in his opinion Joe is just a normally rather active little boy. So how do we know? Is there some *Thing* with a *Name* to it really wrong with our son? Or is he, as our doctor says, just a specially active child?

It's hard to tell without knowing Joe. We can, however, give you some comments from Dr. Stanley Turecki, author of an interesting book called *The Difficult Child*, that may throw some light on the matter. According to Turecki, the term "hyperactive" is used to describe all sorts of behavioral and educational dysfunctions. It is also used to single out one aspect of a child's more complicated behavior—the child's habit of moving around much more than seems "normal."

Among good reasons to question the use (overuse) of the term "hyperactive," according to Turecki, are the following:

1. One characteristic, really an adjective, should not be used to describe a total child.
2. The boundaries of normality are hard to define.
3. The setting of the behavior is very important. This is especially important when the behavior is most evident *only* at school.
4. The age of the child is important. A preschooler is normally much more active than an elementary-school child. Certainly professionals should exercise much more care than most do when diagnosing "hyperactivity."

5. Time of day plays a role. A hungry child may get "hyper" as a result of being hungry.

6. Diet plays a big role. Many mothers have observed their child's adverse reaction to sugary foods or to foods with additives.

If we stop looking at the young child as "hyperactive" and instead think of him as a difficult child with a very high activity level, new horizons open.

And so, says Turecki, we can use the term "hyperactive" for some children, those who are extremely active all the time, who virtually never sit still, whose actions are haphazard rather than goal-directed, who are constantly handling things. It also applies to children who simply can't ever pay attention or follow instructions or who constantly interrupt others.

From what you say about your son at home, it seems as if the term "hyperactive" does not properly apply to him.

YOUNGSTER DOESN'T SEEM WELL EQUIPPED FOR HIS WORK IN THIRD GRADE

Dear Dr. Ames:

Our firstborn is a boy—Eight years old. Oliver is in third grade. Our problem is that he struggles so hard and seems to be getting nowhere fast in his schoolwork. In first grade his teacher called him average and said he got along well with other children and was a joy to have in her class. I felt he was doing poor work, but she passed him to second grade.

In second grade he had trouble reading, and his printing was still bad, but his teacher said that sometimes children "grow up" quickly after a certain age and that he was average and fitted well in his class. He still wrote words backward, including his name, and he missed little words when reading.

This year his printing is better, but his writing is horrible. His arithmetic is bad. He gets upset and cries when he cannot do his work. He still spells words backward. I had a conference with his teacher, and she said he was very slow but was trying hard. I suggested that maybe he had backward vision. She suggested that I take him to an ophthalmologist. I took him and he was given prescription glasses for astigmatism. The doctor thought he was stubborn and immature.

The principal suggested that maybe he just wanted attention. But I disagree, because I think he really tries. He wants to get his homework done so he can enjoy hunting and fishing. Could you tell me if there is a way to find out if he sees backward, or is it too late to find out now? Would it do any good for him to stay next year in third grade? I think he should repeat next year, but my husband thinks he should make his work up this summer and go into fourth grade this fall.

Your husband's plan is all very well but it doesn't take into account the child. From what you say, there seems almost no doubt that Oliver is seriously overplaced in school. We would strongly advise having him do third grade over. If, as we suspect, he is nowhere near ready for fourth grade in the fall, tutoring him this summer would not really solve his problem.

His doing things backward is not in our opinion any sign that he "sees" backward. It is, rather, the way that many Five and one-half and Six-year-old children read, write, and spell. When this backward behavior occurs, it means that a child is at an early level in learning. By recognizing this and giving him work at his own level, he will grow through it. Specific visual aid such as your boy is receiving may help, but even astigmatism is part of growth. Recognizing this, we often do not correct it with special glasses. We would be far more concerned about your son's visual level of maturity, whether he has adequate ocular movements, good depth vision, and flexibility of his visual mechanism. Maybe he needs help through visual training.

At any rate your son may be one who does better in real-life situations than in school. But if he is to be comfortable in school, it seems important for him to go more slowly at his own rate and not be pushed. His papers, which you enclose, confirm our opinion that he is not at this time fully ready to do third-grade work.

MOTHER AND TEACHER UNABLE TO FIND REASON FOR BRIGHT BOY'S INDIFFERENCE

Dear Dr. Ames:

I have a problem with a boy almost Eight years old. Perhaps another mother has the same problem, and I would appreciate having it discussed. Our son, Andrew, is indifferent to everything anybody tells him or tries to teach him. His teacher is almost frantic and so are we. He is indifferent to schoolwork, and at home he is indifferent about the ordinary things everyone has to do. He is healthy and energetic, very intelligent, and hardly ever does anything that could be described as naughty. He talks incessantly and is always thinking seriously, but not about the business he is required to do each moment. He is in a world of his own. How do you penetrate through the barrier such a child puts up?

His teacher says he is capable of being the best student in the class, but he gets a hardly satisfactory mark. The teacher knows that he knows, and so do I. The same with reading—he knows the words but puts on a big act that he doesn't. When it is his turn to read he does halfway well, but when the others read he doesn't follow in his own book and then when the teacher calls on him, he is lost in a dream.

I have given him a motto: Shut your mouth. Stop, look,

and listen to what others are doing and do the same. Think only of the business in front of you and do it right the first time and do it thoroughly, as anything halfway done is not done right and has to be done over. But he won't follow this advice.

If you have an answer, please let me know, as his teacher and I are both desperate to get him to understand.

You and the teacher both feel that Andrew is quite bright enough to do his schoolwork if only he would stop being so indifferent and put his mind to it and try. Thus you, like so many other mothers, are seeking a cure for your child's indifference. However, again like so many other mothers, you have discovered that it is extremely difficult to cure indifference until you have discovered its cause.

The expressions of indifference can be very similar from child to child. They daydream, their minds wander, they seem "lost in a world of their own." They act bored and restless and don't seem to try. Yes, the expressions of indifference are very similar from child to child. But the causes of indifference can be as many as the children concerned.

Indifference can be likened to fever. It is a danger signal, but it can be a sign of any one of dozens of different difficulties. Sometimes a skilled parent can make the necessary diagnosis. But often, even as with a fever, a specialist is needed, both to diagnose and to prescribe. For fever, a physician; for indifference, a child specialist.

Your mottos are good ones, but it is going to take a lot more than a motto to get this little boy on the right track. Is he overplaced in school? Is he with the right teacher? Would his indifference disappear if he could be stimulated through activities that interest him?

The solution is not simple, but the beginnings of answers may probably be found in his own personality makeup. A child specialist should be able to help you better under-

stand this makeup. His problem quite probably lies within normal limits, but it could be severe. That is something that only a specialist who has examined or worked with your son can tell.

ARE PRIMARY SCHOOL TEACHERS FAIR TO LITTLE BOYS?

Dear Dr. Ames:

This may seem like sexism in reverse, but I don't think that primary schools are fair toward little boys. My son, Sammy, started school with such enthusiasm. But now that he is Eight, and in third grade, it's almost as if he had given up. His teacher is always criticizing him. And his self-image is at rock bottom. Is my impression correct that many teachers are not entirely fair to little boys?

Unfortunately it is. Most of us know it, but the problem has been particularly well described in Sheila Moore and Roon Frost's book, *The Little Boy Book.* These authors note that in general boys have a positive outlook at the beginning of school. They believe that if they work hard enough they can do what is necessary to succeed. When asked to rank themselves and others in their classes, both boys and girls who are starting school often place themselves at or near the top.

However, boys and girls as a rule behave very differently from each other. Boys are generally more active than girls. They need to move about and to exercise their large muscles. They require opportunities for blowing off steam. They also tend to be more competitive than girls.

Boys are more exploratory than girls. After a week or less in a classroom, boys can tell you where you keep the cleanser to scrub the sink, which of the window latches has a piece broken off, and how many of the desks are for lefties. They will already have examined the pencil sharpener and may inform you that it is different from the one in the classroom down the hall. (They took that one apart last year.)

Not only are boys different from girls, but teachers tend to respond to children differently, depending on their sex. Boys, being less mature and more active, thus are apt to receive almost as much feedback about their behavior as about their work. Girls hear more about their work itself. Girls act in ways that make it easy for teachers to like them, maintain group control, and keep the classroom neat and orderly. Boys, on the other hand, wiggle, get out of their seats, fiddle with whatever they can get their hands on, and may have trouble staying on task. Neatness and order are relatively unimportant to boys, as is the teacher's opinion of what they do. It is hardly surprising that boys are usually the students who sit out in the hall, stay in at recess, and fill the after-school detention room.

Very few teachers value the ability to run fast, turn on a dime, put mechanical gizmos together right, construct a miniature spaceship out of discarded lumber, or spend the entire afternoon in a ditch to find just the right size frog—skills boys are good at. Instead, teachers value a number of things that are difficult for small boys: writing neatly, keeping quiet, sitting still, reading, and remembering what they were just told to do.

Until he starts primary school, what the child has been asked to do has been tangible and observable. A tower is made from blocks. The child, himself, can judge whether or not he has been successful. On intellectual, school-related tasks, children may be less likely to know what they are aiming for, what they are supposed to do. The result is that first-grade children, especially boys, over time become less certain of their ability or that they will succeed. Over the years, a boy's image of himself in school all too often becomes less positive.

Yes, Mother, you are right. The early school grades tend to be harder for little boys than for little girls.

HOW ABOUT ONE-SEX CLASSES?

Dear Dr. Ames:

In our community, some of the parents are raising the question of single-sex classes in the primary grades. They feel it would be fairer to those many boys who are less mature than girls of the same age and who find it more difficult than the girls to sit still and perform successfully at such tasks as reading and writing. What do you think of all that?

One-sex classes could protect immature and/or not very verbal little boys who find it hard to keep up with the girls. They could allow for classrooms and curriculums to be structured in ways that would be maximally conducive for learning in boys.

While the research on one-sex classrooms is sparse, results available appear positive—not only for boys but for girls as well. Some studies have shown the academic progress of boys in single-sex classes to improve in comparison to boys in mixed-sex groups, in some subject areas. Even though the classes were noisier and the boys less inhibited than in mixed-classes, teachers seemed accepting of males' active behavior without the continued contrast provided by female students. A significant result of one such experiment was a drop in the school's retention rate from 10 percent to 3 percent.

At least one group of researchers suggests that teachers may prefer to teach one sex over the other and may actually do a better job if allowed to teach the preferred sex.

Some investigators raise the question of the validity of some of our beliefs about coeducation. It may or may not be true that boys will be rough if they do not have the "leavening" influence of girls in their school classes. It may or may not be true that females are insufficiently challenged by teachers unless their classes contain an equal number of males.

It *has* been found that gifted high-school girls were more likely to achieve as well as or better than gifted boys in special mathematics classes if they were taught by a woman and the classes enrolled either all girls or a sizable number of girls compared to the number of boys.

In our haste to equalize everything, we may well be overlooking some important ways of enhancing the abilities of children of both sexes.

LEARNING DISABLED OR LEARNING DIFFERENT?

Dear Dr. Ames:

My Eight-year-old son, Steven, has always seemed to me a very smart little boy. And to begin with, he loved school. He did pretty well the first few years except for reading, which has always been hard for him. Steven is especially good at what I consider little boy things—mechanical things, building, space puzzles. My husband and I feel that he has a lot on the ball.

Now he is in third grade and the school is considering putting him into a learning disability class. I don't object to this in theory if it is what he really needs. But somehow I just don't feel that it is.

I agree with you that a school should go very slowly before deciding for sure that a child is learning disabled and belongs in a special class. All too many boys and girls are so labeled and so treated simply because they are, for instance, poor in reading or overplaced. Educator Thomas Armstrong, in his book *In Their Own Way*, has another suggestion.

He strongly recommends that at least in many cases we substitute the concept of *learning differences* as an alternative to *learning disabilities*. His finding, as a learning disability teacher himself, was that millions of children currently being referred to LD classes were actually not handicapped but rather had their own special alternative learning styles that the schools clearly didn't understand. He believes that many boys and girls who appear to underachieve are failing because their unique talents and abilities go unrecognized.

Armstrong gives three examples of children who though labeled by the school as learning disabled were in fact unique learners whose gifts, talents, and abilities had gone unrecognized.

Thus when Billy's mother asked him to figure out the area of a room, using the methods the school taught him, he couldn't do it. But when he was allowed to do it "his way," he succeeded. He explained his way: "Well, when I close my eyes to figure something out, it's like a cross between music and architecture."

Susan was a first-grader who read the encyclopedia for recreation. In class, when asked to write a story about *Little Pig,* a book her class was reading, she wrote, "Little Pig, Little Pig. I'll tell you what you can do with Little Pig."

Marc was an Eleven-year-old dungeon and dragon expert and yet was not doing well in class.

Armstrong's position, and our own, is that the term "learning disability" is not only vastly overused but is incorrectly treated by many educators as a *real thing.* He reminds us that "On Saturday, April 6, 1963, a new disease was invented in Chicago, a disease that, over the next twenty years, would slowly begin to infect millions of school children nationwide. This was no simple virus or common bacteria. It resisted detection by medical personnel, evaded clear diagnosis through testing, *and had no discernible cure.* The Federal government would spend millions of dollars on this affliction over the next twenty years and yet between 1977 and 1983 the number of sufferers would double."*

As Armstrong points out, "It seems a shame to subject persons to the life-long effect of the label 'learning disabled' when we really don't know what it is."

HOW TO HELP THE GIFTED

Dear Dr. Ames:

Would you be good enough to make some comments or to give some advice about our son, Blake? My hus-

* Thomas Armstrong, *In Their Own Way* (Los Angeles, J. P. Tarcher, 1987).

band and I believe that he may be truly gifted but the school doesn't pay much attention to this. Some people act as if we were just boasting when we mention Blake's abilities. Others seem jealous and just change the subject. If there are special things we should be doing for our boy, we would like to know it.

A good start for you, after reading what little I have space to say here, would be to get hold of Priscilla Vail's splendid book *The World of the Gifted Child.* Here are some of the things she, and I, would suggest:

It is unfortunately true that socially the gifted child often seems to start out with a special handicap. The world is apt to view success with a mistrust born of jealousy and to withhold encouragement and acceptance.

Intellectually the gifted child should not march in lock step with everyone else. His mind must not be shackled. His curiosity must be protected and his growth encouraged. But parents and teachers must work hard to help this child strike a happy balance. We should never diminish the child's gifted areas in order to create that balance, but at the same time we should not encourage growth in one area only (the intellectual) or the child will indeed become lopsided.

Parents should avoid the special error of being in awe of their own child. Parents often say, "Oh he's so smart we can't keep up with him." That attitude is bad for children. (And when we say it of Three-and Four-year-olds it is also foolish.) Any child feels safest when his parents are kindly but firmly in charge.

One thing a parent can do is to find counterweights. Thus a child whose genius lies in music may find fascination in mathematics or molecular structure. The child with a gift for history might be fascinated by geology or astronomy. Caretaking is also vital. It can involve smaller children, other people, community projects, plants, or a pet. Responsibility, affection, and being needed contribute powerfully to a positive emotional base. Caretaking forges a needed bond between the gifted child and the rest of the world.

A main rule is: Hold fast to common sense. And remember that giftedness brings its own set of pleasures and perils. Gifted children have intense emotional and social needs that are all too frequently sacrificed to intellectual or academic concerns, particularly when educators get into the act.

Perhaps most important of all, we must keep in mind that there is more to the gifted child than just a brain. And we should also remember that any good done by double promoting such a child in the hopes that his or her intellectual needs will be met tends to be outweighed by the harm of being in a class with boys and girls who are at quite a different stage of development as total people.

Mrs. Vail's own gifted daughter stuck it out in a grade ahead of the one where she as a person would have been comfortable till sixth grade. At the end of this grade, perhaps knowing instinctively what she really needed, she failed four out of six final examinations and met the news with the cheerful statement "Well, I guess I'll just have to stay back." And so "They all grew bosoms together, and though she read the same stories and studied the same history as she had the year before, she brought such different perceptions to those activities that they seemed new."

When teachers tell you that your child is so smart that her or she will figure out social problems even though thrown in with children much older, they're wrong. Even the gifted tend to be more comfortable if they are grouped with others of their own developmental age.

APPENDIXES
appendix a
Books for Eight-Year-Olds

Aardema, Verma. Bringing the Rain to Kapitt Plain. New York: Dial, 1981.

Agee, Jon. Ludlow Laughs. New York: Farrar, Straus & Giroux, 1985.

Allard, Harry. Missy Nelson Has a Field Day. New York: Houghton Mifflin, 1985

Ames, Lee J. Draw 50 Dinosaurs and Other Prehistoric Animals. New York: Doubleday, 1977.

Andersen, Hans Christian. The Snow Queen, translated by Eve La Gallienne. New York: Harper & Row, 1985.

Bagnold, Enid. National Velvet. New York: William Morrow, 1985.

Banks, Lynn Read. The Indian Cupboard. New York: Dell/Avon/Camelot, 1980.

Baskin, Leonard. Leonard Baskin's Miniature Natural History. New York: Pantheon, 1983.

Baum, Frank. The Marvellous Land of Oz. New York: Morrow, 1985.

Berman, Claire G. What Am I Doing in a Stepfamily? New York: Lyle Stuart, 1982.

Brown, Heywood. The Fifty-first Dragon. Englewood Cliffs, NJ: Prentice Hall, 1968.

Caines, Jeanette. Chilly Stomach. New York: Harper & Row, 1986.

Cleary, Beverly. RAMONA FOREVER. New York: Morrow, 1984.

———. THE MOUSE AND THE MOTORCYCLE. New York: Dell—A Yearling Book, 1985.

Cole, Joanne. DOCTOR CHANGE. New York: Morrow, 1986.

Coville, Bruce, and Coville, Katherine. SARAH'S UNICORN. New York: Harper & Row, 1985.

Dahl, Roald. THE WITCHES. New York: Puffin Books/Penguin, 1979.

———. THE BFG. New York: Puffin Books/Penguin, 1985.

———. THE GIRAFFE AND THE PELLY AND ME. New York: Farrar, Straus and Giroux, 1985.

———. FANTASTIC MR. FOX. New York: Knopf, 1986.

Duvoisin, Roger. SNOWY AND WOODY. New York: Knopf, 1979.

Freschet, Bernice. OWL IN THE GARDEN. New York: Lothrop, Lee and Shepard, 1985.

Gage, Wilson. MRS. GADDY AND THE FAST-GROWING VINE. New York: Greenwillow, 1985.

Gerstein, Mordicai. TALES OF PAN. New York: Harper & Row, 1986.

Grollman, Earl A. TALKING ABOUT DEATH: A DIALOGUE BETWEEN PARENT AND CHILD (new ed.). Boston: Beacon Press, 1976.

Hall, Donald. RIDDLE RAT. New York: Warne, 1977.

Hastings, Belina. SIR GAWAIN AND THE LOATHLY LADY. New York: Lothrop, Lee and Shepard, 1985.

Hoban, Lillian, and Hoban, Phoebe. THE LAZIEST ROBOT IN ZONE ONE: AN I CAN READ BOOK. New York: Harper & Row, 1983.

Hughes, Frieda. GETTING RID OF AUNT EDNA. New York: Harper & Row, 1986.

Hughes, Shirley. CHIPS AND JESSIE. New York: Lothrop, Lee and Shepard, 1986.

Keller, Charles. ASTRONAUTS: SPACE JOKES AND RIDDLES. Englewood Cliffs, NJ: Prentice Hall, 1983.

Kellogg, Steven. TALLYHO, PINKERTON. New York: Dial, 1982.

Kessler, Leonard. THE WORST TEAM EVER. New York: Greenwillow, 1985.

Kipling, Rudyard. JUST SO STORIES. New York: Doubleday, 1946.

Lennett, Robin. IT'S OK TO SAY NO. New York: Tom Doherty Associates, 1986.

Lester, Julius. THE TALES OF UNCLE REMUS. New York: Dutton, 1987.

Lexau, Joan. THE HOMEWORK CAPER: AN I CAN READ BOOK. New York: Harper & Row, 1985

Lionni, Leo. FREDERICK'S FABLES: A LEO LIONNI TREASURY OF FAVORITE STORIES. New York: Pantheon, 1985.

Mannes, Stephen. CHICKEN TREK. New York: Dutton, 1987.

Martin, Eva. TALES OF THE FAR NORTH. New York: Dutton, 1987.

Mayle, Peter. WHERE DID I COME FROM? New York: Lyle Stuart, 1978.

Mebs, Gudrun. SUNDAY CHILD. New York: Dutton, 1986.

Milne, A. A. WHEN WE WERE VERY YOUNG. New York: Dutton, 1985.

Parish, Peggy, MERRY CHRISTMAS AMELIA BEDELIA. New York: Greenwillow, 1986.

Paterson, Katherine. THE MASTER PUPPETEER. New York: Dell/Avon/Camelot, 1981.

Powzyk, Joyce. WALLABY CREEK. New York: Lothrop, Lee and Shepard, 1985.

Resen, Michael. DON'T PUT MUSTARD IN THE CUSTARD. New York: Dutton, 1986.

Sadler, Marilyn. ALISTAIR IN OUTER SPACE. Englewood Cliffs, NJ: Prentice Hall, 1985.

Sattler, Helen Roney. PTEROSAURS, THE FLYING REPTILES. New York: Lothrop, Lee and Shepard, 1985.

Schwartz, Alvin. THERE IS A CARROT IN MY EAR AND OTHER NOODLE TALES. New York: Harper & Row, 1982.

Simon, Seymour. BITS AND BYTES: A COMPUTER DICTIONARY FOR BEGINNERS. New York: Crowell Junior Books, 1985.

Slate, Alfred. THE TROUBLE ON JANUS. New York: Lippincott Junior Books, 1985.

appendix b
Books for Parents
of Eight-Year-Olds

Ames Louise Bates. Is Your Child in the Wrong Grade? Rosemont, NJ: Modern Learning Press, 1978.

————. What Am I Doing in This Grade? New York: Programs for Education, 1985.

————. Straight Answers to Parents' Questions. New York: Clarkson Potter, 1988.

————, Metraux, Ruth W., Rodell, Janet L., and Walker, Richard N. Child Rorschach Responses. New York: Brunner/Mazel, rev. ed., 1974.

Armstrong, Thomas. In Their Own Way. New York: Jeremy P. Tarcher/St. Martin's Press, 1985.

Berman, Claire. Making It as a Stepparent: New Roles, New Rules. New York: Doubleday, 1980.

————. What Am I Doing in This Stepfamily? New York: Lyle Stuart, 1982.

Calladine, Andrew, and Calladine, Carole. One Terrific Year: Supporting Your Child Through the Ups and Downs of Their Year. Minneapolis, MN: Winston Press, 1985.

Comer, James P., and Pouissaint, Alvin F. Black Child Care: How to Bring Up a Healthy Black Child in America. New York: Pocket Books, 1980.

Crook, William G. Tracking Down Hidden Food Allergy. Jackson, TN: Professional Books, 1980.

————, and Stevens, Laura J. Solving the Puzzle of the

HARD TO RAISE CHILD. Jackson, TN: Professional Books/ Random House, 1987.

Dodson, Fitzhugh. How to Parent. New York: New American Library, 1973.

————. How to Discipline with Love. New York: Rawson, 1978.

————. How to Single Parent. New York: Harper & Row, 1987.

Feingold, Ben. Why Your Child Is Hyperactive. New York: Random House, 1974.

Ferber, Richard. "The Child Who Doesn't Sleep." In Schiff, Eileen (ed.) Experts Advise Parents. New York: Delacorte, 1987.

Forer, Lucille. The Birth Order Factor. New York: McKay, 1976.

Gardner, Howard. Frames of Mind. New York: Basic Books, 1983.

Gesell, Arnold, Ilg, Frances L., and Ames, Louise B. The Child from Five to Ten (rev. ed.). New York: Harper & Row, 1977.

Goldstein, Sonja, and Solnit, Albert. Divorce and Your Child: Practical Suggestions for Parents. New Haven, CT: Yale University Press, 1984.

Grant, Jim. I Hate School. Rosemont, NJ: Programs for Education, 1986.

Grollman, Earl A., and Sweder, Gerri. The Working Parent Dilemma: How to Balance the Responsibility of Children and Career. Boston: Beacon Press, 1986.

Healy, Jane M. Your Child's Growing Mind. New York: Doubleday, 1987.

Ilg, Franches L., Ames, Louise B., and Baker, Sidney M. Child Behavior (rev. ed.). New York: Harper & Row, 1981.

Kramer, Rita. In Defense of the Family: Raising Children in America Today. New York: Basic Books, 1983.

Lanski, Vicki. BIRTHDAY PARTIES. New York: Bantam Books, 1986.

Lerman, Saf. PARENT AWARENESS TRAINING: POSITIVE PARENTING FOR THE 1980s. New York: A & W Publishers, 1980.

Matthews, Sanford J., and Brinley, Maryann B. THROUGH THE MOTHERHOOD MAZE. New York: Doubleday, 1982.

Melina, Lois R. RAISING ADOPTED CHILDREN. Moscow, ID: Solstice Press, 1986.

Moore, Sheila, and Frost, Roon. THE LITTLE BOY BOOK. New York: Clarkson N. Potter/Crown, 1986.

Pitcher, Evelyn Goodenough, and Schultz, Lynn Hickey. BOYS AND GIRLS AT PLAY: THE DEVELOPMENT OF SEX ROLES. South Hadley, MA: Bergin & Harvey, 1983.

Procaccini, Joseph, and Kiefaber, Mark W. P.L.U.S. PARENTING: TAKE CHARGE OF YOUR FAMILY. New York: Doubleday, 1985.

Rapp, Doris J. ALLERGIES AND THE HYPERACTIVE CHILD. New York: Sovereign Books/Simon & Schuster, 1980.

Scarr, Sandra. MOTHER CARE OTHER CARE. New York: Basic Books, 1984.

Schiff, Eileen (ed.). EXPERTS ADVISE PARENTS. New York: Delacorte, 1987.

Smith, Lendon, FEED YOUR KIDS RIGHT. New York: McGraw-Hill, 1979.

Smith, Sally L. NO EASY ANSWERS: TEACHING THE LEARNING DISABLED CHILD. Boston: Little, Brown, 1979.

Stein, Sara Bonnet. GIRLS AND BOYS: THE LIMITS OF NON-SEXIST CHILD REARING. New York: Scribners, 1985.

Stevens, Laura J., Stevens, George E., and Stoner, Rosemary. HOW TO FEED YOUR HYPERACTIVE CHILD. New York: Doubleday, 1972.

Trelease, Jim. THE READ-ALOUD HANDBOOK. New York: Penguin, 1985.

Turecki, Stanley, and Tonner, Leslie. THE DIFFICULT CHILD. New York: Putnam, 1985.

Vail, Priscilla L. THE WORLD OF THE GIFTED CHILD. New York: Walker, 1985.

———. SMART KIDS WITH SCHOOL PROBLEMS. New York: Dutton, 1987.

Visher, Emily, and Visher, John. HOW TO WIN AS A STEPFAMILY. New York: Dembner/Norton, 1982.

Wunderlich, Ray C., and Kalita, Dwight K. NOURISHING YOUR CHILD. New Canaan, CT: Keats, 1984.

NOTES

1. Crook, William G. SOLVING THE PROBLEM OF THE HARD TO RAISE CHILD. New York: Random House, 1987.
2. Galland, Leo. SUPERIMMUNITY FOR KIDS. New York: Dutton, 1988.
3. Smith, Lendon. FEED YOUR KIDS RIGHT. New York: McGraw-Hill, 1979.
4. Wunderlich, Ray C., and Kalita, Dwight K. NOURISHING YOUR CHILD. New Canaan, CT: Keats, 1984.
5. Gesell, Arnold, Ilg, Frances L., and Ames, Louise Bates. THE CHILD FROM FIVE TO TEN, rev. ed. New York: Harper & Row, 1977.
6. Pitcher, Evelyn Goodenough, and Schultz, Lynn Hickey. BOYS AND GIRLS AT PLAY: THE DEVELOPMENT OF SEX ROLES. South Hadley, MA: Bergen & Harvey, 1983, p. 153.
7. Stein, Sara Bonnet. GIRLS AND BOYS: THE LIMITS OF NON-SEXIST CHILD REARING. New York: Scribners, 1985, p. 189.
8. Grant, Jim. I HATE SCHOOL. Rosement, NJ: Programs for Education, 1986. p. 41.

INDEX